TABLE OF CONTENTS

INTRODUCTION

Excel is a very powerful application that offers countless opportunities to improve and track the efficiency of our daily tasks. Designed to improve the storing, analysis, and calculations of large sets of data, Excel has the potential to boost work productivity and efficiency for the knowledgeable user massively.

It is disheartening to witness how many people view excel only as a data storage tool, where each data point is manually typed—a brainless task that consumes countless hours of your day.

There are many reasons you need to learn the basic skills in excel software. Excel is a basic tool, and you need to have a basic idea of it. Having a basic idea of this important tool will help you in your personal and professional life.

Excel now has many teamwork features that can help you get things done no matter where your employees are based. MS Office is a truly global collection of tools. With Excel, we can share spreadsheets and have managers or team members add data, modify formulas, alter or add charts, and change existing cells and formatting. You can then monitor and manage the changes, accept or reject cell changes, and add comments to data cells as required.

The possibilities of working on a sheet with other colleagues are limitless with Office 365, which is now being rolled out to a big number of businesses. Collaboration through the internet is the way to go!

Excel allows users to generate anything from quick collections and basic arithmetic formulas, interact with external sources, and analyze millions of documents. In milliseconds, complex engineering equations and statistics may be done. Repeated spreadsheet operations may be streamlined and completed with a simple mouse click.

You can quickly produce professional-looking budgets, surveys, forecasts, invoices, tables, maps, matrices, and practically every other kind of artifact containing language, money, numeric, or time values using formatting, graphs, and other presentation methods.

Who Is This Book For

This book is for those who want to master a new skill, namely a full understanding of Microsoft Excel, but it will also push them to practice enough to master this ability. So, you'll be learning and practicing different concepts, functions, and formulas that you'll use later in your social, professional, or academic life.

This book would be a perfect guide for you. In this book, the following topics about MS Excel will be covered. Custom solutions must maintain a competitive edge and optimize revenues in the complex business climate.

This Excel Guide compiles all required how-to information for utilizing the current version of Microsoft Excel's many functionalities. This book strives to be of help to all users, regardless of what and how experience they have with the software. It is written in a straightforward, easy-to-understand manner.

This book is aimed at people who want:

- To spare time and effort as well as increase productivity in Excel

- Powerful shortcuts in their worksheets so they don't have to use the Excel ribbon continually

- To avoid doing unnecessary, mundane, repetitive tasks every day

- To manipulate data in their worksheets quickly and easily without having to use complicated formulas

- To quickly create Excel's more powerful features such as pivot tables and charts and manipulate them with a click of a button

- To automate their worksheets

- When you're finished, you'll have a good understanding of Excel and be able to move forward to the next level of your Microsoft Office suite learning

MODULE A

CHAPTER 1: EXCEL OVERVIEW

Microsoft Office Latest Versions Overview

There have been 30 different versions of Excel, starting from 1985 up to this present day. Currently, the most used versions are Excel 2016, 2019, 365, 2020, and the latest Excel 2021.

All these versions of Excel are different from each other, and their differences cut across both Windows and Macs. The versions are stated below:

- Excel 2020
- Excel 365
- Excel 2019
- Excel 2016 and 365
- Excel 2013 (Windows)
- Excel 2011 (Mac)

- Excel 2010 (Windows)
- Excel 2008 (2011)
- Excel 2007 (Windows)
- Excel 2004 (Mac)
- Excel 2003 (Windows)

- Older Windows versions are 2002, 2000, 97, 95, 4.0, 3.0, and 2.0
- Older Mac versions are 2001, 2000, 98, 5, 4, 3, 2 and 1
- OS/2 versions are 2.2, 2.3 and 3

The new version, Excel 2021, has been recently launched. At the time I'm publishing this book, the best two options for you to get Excel for your personal use:

1) OFFICE HOME & STUDENT 2021. This is a permanent license, as a one-time purchase for a lifetime license for your device, 1 PC or Mac, for $149.99 USD. This includes:

- Excel, Word, and PowerPoint (classic 2021 versions)
- 60 days of Microsoft support (no additional cost)
- Compatible with Windows 10, Windows 11, and Mac OS
- Use for non-commercial purposes
- Compatible with Microsoft Teams

2) MICROSOFT 365. This is a paid subscription that makes sure you always have the most up-to-date modern productivity tools from Microsoft. So you will always have the latest Excel version at your disposal. You have two options:

• Single User, Microsoft 365 Personal, for $69.99/year or $6.99/month

• Multiple Users, Microsoft 365 Family, for $99.99/year or $9.99/month

They both give you access to all Office apps (Word, Excel, PowerPoint, OneNote, Outlook, One Drive, Family Safety, Skype) + Free 1 TB OneDrive storage per person (one for Personal package up to 6 for Family package). With both options, you can:

a.   Access smart assistance features, plus hundreds of premium templates, photos, icons, and fonts in Word, Excel, and PowerPoint

b.   Use OneDrive to share and save files

c.   Take advantage of the advanced security of OneDrive and Outlook

d.   Get support via chat or phone (no additional cost)

Only with Microsoft 365 Family you can:

a.   Set location alerts in the Microsoft Family Safety mobile app*

b.   Each person can use the subscription on up to 5 devices at the same time

c.   App available for free

Here below, you can find a tab to quickly check all the options described above. I would recommend you to visit the following web page to purchase one of the Office packages or just to have more information about them. https://www.microsoft.com/en-us/microsoft-365/buy/compare-all-microsoft-365-products

	Microsoft 365 Family	Microsoft 365 Personal	Office Home & Student 2021 One-time purchase for PC and Mac
Usage	2-6 people	1 person	1 PC or Mac
Word, Excel, PowerPoint, OneNote	Premium	Premium	Classic
OneDrive cloud storage to back up files and photos	Up to 6TB (1TB per person)	1TB	
Teams	✔	✔	
Microsoft Family Safety mobile app1	Premium		
Outlook	Premium	Premium	
Works on Windows, macOS, iOS, and Android	✔	✔	
Advanced security for email and files	✔	✔	
Ongoing technical support	✔	✔	

How To Launch Excel

To begin, we'll first review different ways to open our Excel program.

Using desktop shortcut. Look for the Excel software shortcut icon on your desktop and double-click it to start Excel. Icons may vary depending on the version of Excel that you have installed. Below are the most recent ones.

If you cannot locate an Excel shortcut on your desktop, create one with the easy steps below.

Look for the Excel executable file in the installation location on your PC. Inside the Microsoft Office installation folder, look for the Excel executable file. Depending on the version of Office you are using, the default installation location differs.

Usually, the Excel executable files are in the directories similar to these below.

64-bit Windows: C:\Program Files\Microsoft Office\Office21\

32-bit Windows: C:\Program Files (x86)\Microsoft Office\Office21\

After locating the Excel executable file, right-click it (EXCEL.EXE) and choose *Send to > Desktop*. This will create a shortcut on your desktop that should look like this one below.

Using the Start menu. Click the *'Start'* (Windows) button, scroll to the letter *'E'*, and select the program Excel.

Excel Startup Screen

When you Excel, the program will display the default *Start*up screen, similar to this one here below. This screen was introduced in the version 2013

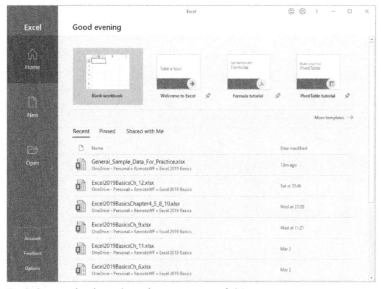

Let's have a look at the relevant parts of this screen.

Workbook

As a first thing in the *Start*up screen, you will notice the *Blank Workbook, which* is a single file that contains one or more spreadsheets, often known as worksheets. We will look at all the worksheets parts later. For now, it's important that you know that a workbook is essentially an Excel file. It is the equivalent of a binder with lots of drawing sheets for an artist.

New button

Here you can create a blank workbook. Just click on the icon in the upper left corner.

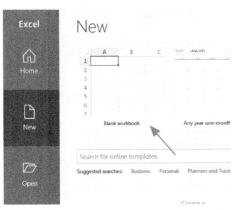

Alternatively, you can start a new workbook from premade Excel templates, which are very useful. We will see how to use them later on the next pages.

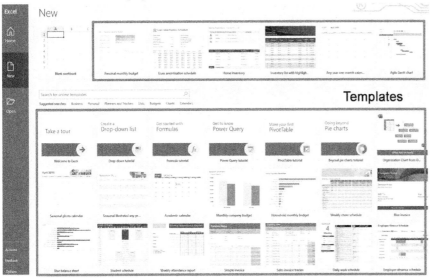

Open button

In this section, you can mainly go to find any workbook on your PC and open it. As well are shown recent workbooks that you have been working with.

The Excel User Interface

This section provides an overview of the Excel user interface so that you're familiar with the names of various parts of the interface that will be mentioned throughout the book.

Once you open a blank workbook, an existing one, or any of the templates at your disposal, you will now into the Excel user interface, which you can see here below,

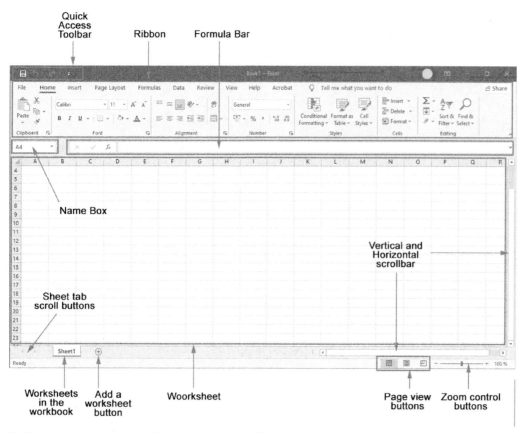

Let's go now to discover the main parts of which it is composed

Quick Access Toolbar.

This is an area where you can add commands that you can quickly access, hence the name.

Ribbon

The ribbon in Excel is divided into four major categories: Tabs, Group, Buttons, and Dialog Box launcher. They are divided based on their functions or categories.

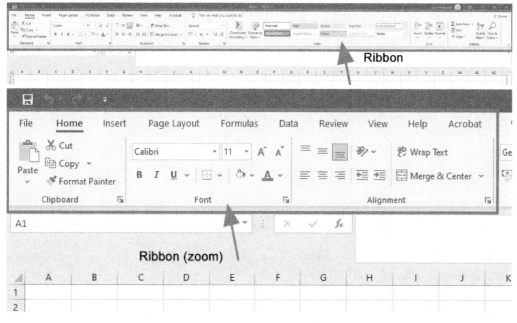

Let's take a closer look at it!

The Ribbon Tabs

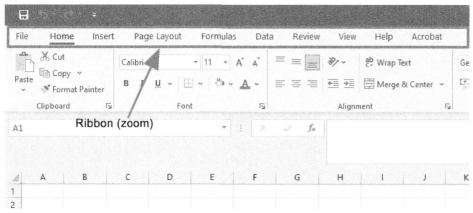

Ribbon (zoom)

These are a group of commands arranged according to their functions from *the File menu* to *Add-ins*.

File tab: opens the user view when clicked. The Backstage view, similar to the *Start*up screen, has several menu options, including Home, New, Open, Info, Save, Save As, Print, Share, Export, Publish, and Close. At the bottom of the list, you have the Account menu option where you view your user information. You also have options where you can change many of Excel's default settings.

Note that if your Excel workbook is saved on OneDrive, and you have *AutoSave* set to *On*, you'll not see the *Save As* menu option; instead, you'll have to *Save* a copy in its place.

To exit the Backstage view, click on the back button (the left-pointing arrow at the top-left of the page).

Home tab: The *Home* tab provides the most used set of commands. The other tabs provide command buttons for specific tasks like inserting objects into your spreadsheet, formatting the page layout, working with formulas, working with datasets, reviewing your spreadsheet, etc.

Insert tab: The Insert tab is used to add objects such as charts, PivotTables, images, hyperlinks, special symbols, equations, 3D models, shapes, header, footer, etc., to the worksheet.

Page layout tab: This tab contains options or tools that manage the worksheet's appearance both on the screen and for printing. These options manage the theme settings, page margins, gridlines, object aligning, and print area.

Formulas tab: This contains tools for inserting and troubleshooting functions. This is also used to define and control the calculation options.

Data tab: This contains commands like filtering, sorting, and manipulating data that are used in managing data on the worksheet. This tab also allows for the importing of data from external sources.

Review tab: This tab allows you to check errors in spelling, track changes, share and protect Excel worksheets and workbooks.

View tab: this contains commands such as switching between worksheets views, freezing panes, arranging multiples windows, *etc.*

Help: This tab gives you access to **the Help Task Pane** to get in touch with Microsoft support for any help regarding the use of Excel.

Developer: This allows access to advanced Excel features such as VBA macros, ActiveX, *etc.* By default, it is hidden, and you need to enable it first to have access to it.

Add-ins: This only appears when an older workbook is opened or when an add-in is installed to customize the toolbar.

The Ribbon Groups

The *Ribbon* Groups contains tools such as buttons, sub-menus, and dialog box.

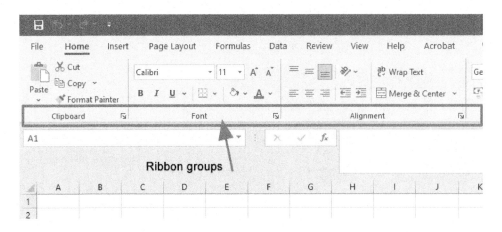

The Command Buttons

These are tools in the *Ribbon* groups that are used to run a command or perform a particular function.

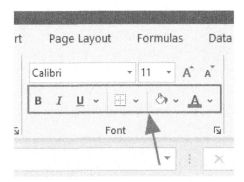

The Dialogue Box Launcher

The *Dialog Box Launcher* is a diagonal arrow in the lower-right corner of some groups. When clicked, it opens a dialog box containing additional command options related to that group. So, if you cannot see a command on the *Ribbon* for a task you want to carry out, click on the small dialog box launcher to display more options for that group. This is located at the right bottom corner of the *Ribbon* groups. When you click on the Dialog Box launcher button, the full features on the *Ribbon* groups are displayed.

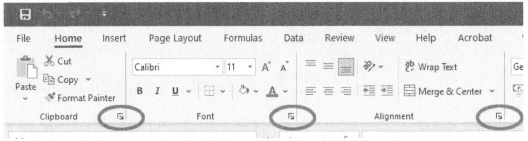

Customizing the Ribbon

The area of the screen containing the tabs and command buttons is called the *Ribbon*. You can customize the *Ribbon* to your liking by adding or removing tabs and command buttons.

To customize the *Ribbon*, right-click anywhere on the *Ribbon*, below the tabs, and select *Customize the Ribbon…* from the pop-up menu.

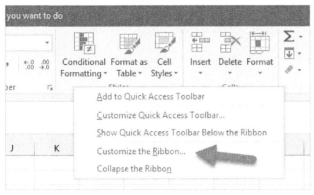

This will open the *Excel Options* window.

In the *Excel Options* window, the *Customize Ribbon* page will be selected, and on that page, you have two main boxes. On the right, you have the box that shows your current tabs - *Main Tabs*. On the left, you have the command buttons that you can add to the *Ribbon*.

To expand a group in the *Main Tabs* box, click on the plus sign (+) to the left of an item.

To find commands that are not currently on your *Ribbon*, click the down arrow on the left box (named *Choose commands from*) and select *Commands Not in the Ribbon* from the drop-down list.

You will see a list of commands that are not on your *Ribbon*. This is useful as it filters out the commands that are already on your *Ribbon*.

Note: You cannot add or remove the default commands on the *Ribbon*, but you can uncheck them on the list to prevent them from being displayed. Also, you cannot add command buttons to the default groups. You must create a new group to add a new command button.

To create a custom group: Select the tab in which you want to create the group. This could be one of the default tabs or the new one you've created. This will create a new group within the currently selected tab. Select the new group and click on *Rename* to give the group your preferred name. You now have a custom group in which you can add commands.

To add commands to your custom group:

Select your custom group in the list on the right side of the screen.

Select the new command button you want to add from the list on the left side of the screen.

Select the command on the right box and click << *Remove*.

Click *OK* to confirm the change.

When you view the customized tab on the *Ribbon*, you'll see your new group and the command buttons you've added.

Formula Bar
This is where you'll see the cell value, computations, or formula. We'll learn more as we start learning about formulas in the next pages

Cell Address
A cell address, also known as a cell reference, is a combination of a column letter and a row number that is used to identify a cell on a worksheet. For example, B2 denotes the cell at the intersection of column B and row 2

Excel Worksheet
The worksheet is the collection of organized cells in rows and columns. This is where data such as labels, values, and formulas are entered.

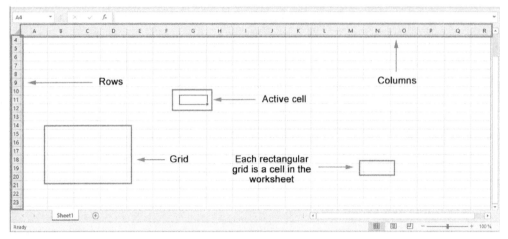

Page view buttons
The primary function of the view buttons is to provide a display view of the page or file. There are three buttons: "Normal," "Page Layout," and "Page Break Preview." The default view of a worksheet is "Normal."

Worksheets Buttons
In the left bottom hand, you can find the label with the name of the worksheet where you are currently working (worksheets in the workbook) and a button with a "+" sign to add a new worksheet to your workbook.

To move from one workbook to another, click on the workbook name you want to work in.

Cell Address
This box's known as Name Box, too, and it allows you to assign a name to any cell you want.

Quick Access Toolbar (QAT)
The *Quick Access Toolbar (QAT)* contains a set of predefined or commonly used commands. By default, this toolbar is located in the upper left-hand corner of the user interface, and it contains three buttons: Save, Undo, and Redo.

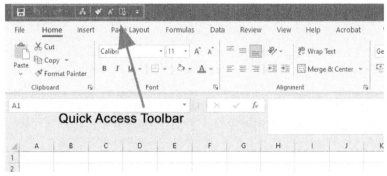

How to customize the Quick Access Toolbar and the Ribbon
The *QAT* commands always remain active regardless of which ribbon is active, so I find it more efficient to modify the *Quick Access Toolbar.* However, you may prefer to change the *Ribbon.*

So, let's see how we can add a button to both the *Quick Access Toolbar* and *Ribbon.*

First of all, click the drop-down arrow on the *QAT,* and select *More Commands…*

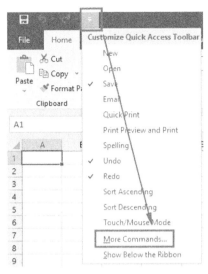

#1: *Select either* Quick Access Toolbar or Customize Ribbon

Note: Alternatively, you may right-click over the *Ribbon* or the *Quick Access Toolbar* to receive the below dialog box:

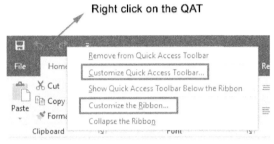

#2: Select a command you would like to add

#3: Select the *'Add>>'* button

#4: Click the *'OK'* button

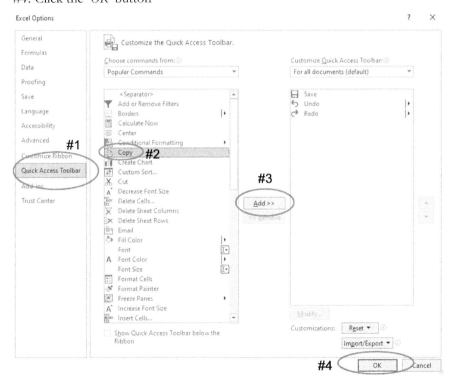

As you can add buttons, you can also remove them. The procedure is the same, so click the drop-down arrow on the *Quick Access Toolbar, and* select More Commands…

Select either Quick Access Toolbar or Customize Ribbon

#1: Select a command you would like to remove

#2: Select the *'<<Remove'* button

#3: Click the *'OK'* button

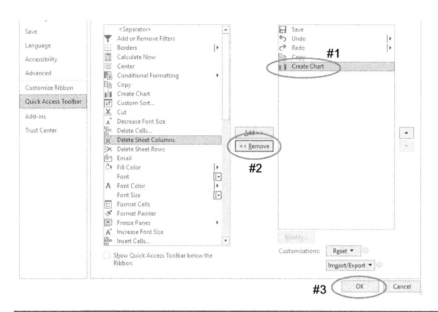

Excel Workbook

Creating a New Excel Workbook

Launch Excel from the *Start* menu or the icon you have created on your taskbar or desktop.

Excel will launch to the *Home* screen. The Excel 2020 start screen enables you to create a new blank workbook or open one of your recently opened workbooks. You also have a selection of predefined templates that you can use as the basis of your workbook.

To create a new workbook, click on *Blank workbook*. This will create a new workbook with a worksheet named *Sheet1*.

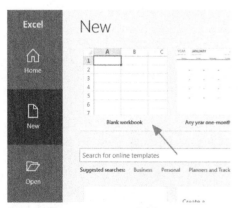

Tip: Another way to quickly create a new workbook when you already have a workbook open is to press *CTRL + N* on your keyboard. This will create a new workbook.

Create A Workbook Based on A Template. To create a new workbook based on one of Excel's predefined templates, click on the *New* button on the left navigation pane to go to the New screen. The categories of available templates are listed on the top of the screen next to *Suggested searches*.

You can narrow down the displayed templates by clicking on one of the categories - Business, Personal, Planners and Trackers, Lists, Budgets, Charts, or Calendars.

Once you identify the template you'd like to use, double click on it to create a new worksheet based on it.

Open an Existing Workbook

In case you already have a file that you want to open in Excel, being in the user interface, you can just press CTRL + O. This combination will open the file dialog box.

On the *Open* page of the Backstage view, you'll see the following options:

Recent: To open a recent workbook, select *Recent* and click on the workbook you want to open on the right.

OneDrive - Personal: To open a workbook from OneDrive, click on *OneDrive - Personal* and select your file from the right. Please note that if you're not in the root folder of OneDrive, you can use the blue up-arrow to navigate to the folder that contains your workbook.

This PC: To open a workbook from the Documents local folder on your PC, click on *This PC* to display the Documents folder. Navigate to the folder containing your workbook. Click on the file to open it.

Browse: To browse for a file on your computer, click the *Browse* button, look at the file you want to open, select the file, and click on the *Open* button.

On the other hand, you can find and open an existing workbook by clicking on the *File* tab on the *Ribbon*, and then click on the *Open* option (same thing if you are launching Excel), and then you can start browsing for the files that you want to work on it.

Note: Excel files often end with the file extension(s) .XLS (for workbooks created using older versions of Excel) and/or.XLSX (for workbooks created using newer versions).

Saving Your Excel Workbook

To save your workbook for the first time:

Click the disk icon on the *Quick Access Toolbar* (the top-left of the window) or click on the *File* tab, and this will open the Backstage view.

Click *Save As* (you'll see *Save a Copy* if your file has been previously saved to OneDrive).

On the next screen, click on *OneDrive – Personal* (if you're using OneDrive) or *This PC* (if you're not saving it to OneDrive).

If you want to save it to a folder/sub-folder, navigate to the folder by double-clicking on the folder.

Click on the *Save* button to save the workbook.

You'll be taken back to the *Home* tab after the file has been saved.

Note: If your workbook has been previously saved to OneDrive or SharePoint and *AutoSave* is set to on, you'll have to *Save a Copy* in place of *Save As*. You can use Save a Copy to save your workbook as a different file.

When you save a file, it overwrites the prior version. If you want to keep an old version of the file while continuing to work on it, then you need to use *Save As* (or *Save a Copy*) as described above. This would save the workbook you're working on as a new file while the old version remains unchanged.

Tip: For a quicker way to save your workbook, after the first save, you can use the *CTRL + S* shortcut keys. For a list of the most frequently used shortcuts in Excel, see the Appendix.

Close a Workbook Ensure you've saved the workbook (if you want to keep the changes).

Click on *File* to display the Backstage view, and then click *Close*.

Or Press the *CTRL+W* shortcut keys to close the workbook.

Closing Your Workbook and Closing Excel

To close a currently open workbook, you can press the *CTRL+W*. This will leave Excel in a workbook-less state, which will disable most of its functions aside from a few menu and ribbon options.

You can also close the workbook by clicking the *File* tab and then clicking on the *Close* button on the left side.

If you want to close Excel together with the workbook, you can just press *Alt+F4*. Alternatively, you can just click on the *Exit* button in the upper right corner of your screen ("X" symbol).

How To Remove the Gridlines and others Elements From Your Worksheet

The gridlines are the lines on the Excel worksheet which help divide the cells from each other within a worksheet. The gridlines help to separate and organize the data accordingly in a way that can be clearly seen and understood. You can choose to remove the gridlines, and to do this, follow the simple steps below.

Click on the View tab

Click on Gridlines to effect changes

Note: As you can see, with the same process, you could hide the *Formula* bar and the *Headings* as well.

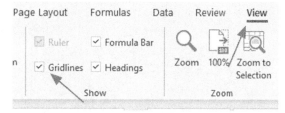

When the gridlines are removed from the worksheet, your worksheet will look like the image of the worksheet shown below.

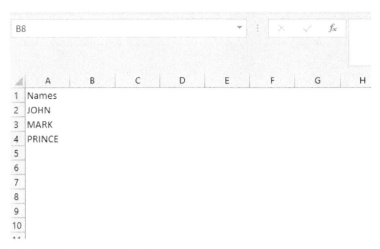

Columns Rows, and Cells

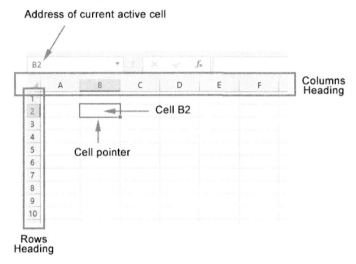

Columns and Rows are aligned cells. The columns are vertical and marked with the alphabet letters (*Columns Heading*), while the rows are horizontal and marked with numbers (*Row Heading*).

Cells are little rectangular boxes on the worksheet where you enter the data by clicking on them. A cell is formed by the junction of a row and a column. Every worksheet is made up of a thousand cells, and each of them is identified by row number and column header such as A1, A2, and so on.... This is called *Cell Address* or *Cell Name*.

Active Cell

An active cell is also known as the *cell pointer* or the *chosen cell*. An activated cell is a cell in edit mode, which means that you can enter data, modify an existing value, and so on.

To activate a cell, just left-click on it. Remember that only one cell can be activated at a time, and you can easily detect it because it is surrounded by a thick border (*Cell Pointer*).

Border in excel

Adding borders in excel can help you to distinguish different sections, emphasize certain data such as column heading or rows and make your work look presentable. Without borders, an excel worksheet can be difficult to read because of its complex structure. A border is a line that surrounds a cell. The cell border is used to accent specific sections of the spreadsheet to make them stand out.

 Cell border

The border does not appear by default; you need to apply it manually. We will have a look in-depth in the next pages

CHAPTER 2: EXCEL FUNDAMENTALS

Data

Entering Data

There is more than one way to do this. Following you can find the two easier ways.

Type your data directly into a cell. Click in the cell where you want to enter your data and start to type in.

Using the Formula bar. This is can really help if you are typing in a large text. Select your cell and type the data into the formula bar, it will automatically appear on the selected cell.

Copying and Pasting Data

Quick copy and paste:

On the *Home* tab, *Clipboard* group, click on *Copy* (this is the double paper icon next to the Paste command).

Click on the first cell of the area where you want to paste the contents, and click on *Paste*.

To speed up this process, you could use the same procedure but replacing with *CTRL+C* combination the *Copy* button and *CTRL+V* the *Paste* one.

The marquee remains active to let you know that you can carry on pasting the copied content if you wish to paste it in multiple areas.

To get rid of the marquee hit the *ESC* key.

Other pasting options:

To access other pasting options, after copying data, on the toolbar, click the *Paste* command button to display a pop-up menu with several pasting options.

You can mouse over the options to see what each one does.

You also see a preview of the paste action on your worksheet.

For example, if you want to paste the contents and the column width, you would select the option that says *Keep Source Width (W)*.

This is on the second row of the menu.

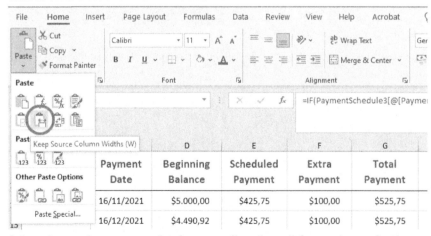

Select that option to paste the data as well as the cell formatting and column width.

Once done, remove the marquee around the copied range by hitting the *ESC* key. This tells Excel that you're done with the copying.

Moving Data

To move content, you follow a similar set of actions as we did with copying; however, you would *Cut* the data instead of *Copy* it.

Select the range you want to move.

On the *Home* tab, click on the *Cut* button (this is the command with the scissors icon), or press *CTRL+X*. A scrolling marquee will appear around the area you've chosen to cut.

Place your cursor on the first cell of the area where you want to paste the content. You only need to select one cell.

Click on *Paste* on your toolbar. This will move the content from its current location and place it in the area you've chosen.

The cut and paste action automatically copy the format of the cells across but not the width. So, you need to adjust the width of the cells if necessary.

Find and Replace Data

A worksheet can have over a million rows of data, for example, so it may be difficult to locate specific information. Excel provides a *Find and Replace* feature that enables you to quickly find data in your worksheet and replace it if needed. If you have used the find function in other Microsoft Office applications before, then you should be familiar with this feature. By pressing *CTRL+F*, the following dialog box will be displayed.

The *Find what* field contains the value you want to find. In the example below is the word "Hello." Then click on *Find All*, and the following will be the result.

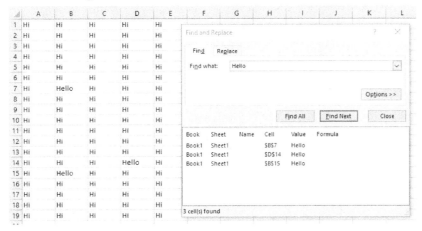

You can click on the *Options* button to display more options to narrow down your search.

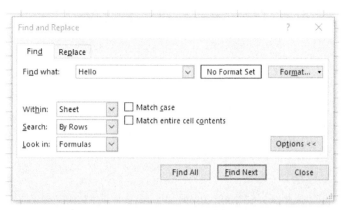

Within allows you to search the current worksheet or the whole workbook.

Search allows you to search by rows (default) or columns.

Look in is used to search cell formulas, values, or comments. The default is formulas, so to look for values, change this option to Values from the drop-down list.

Match case, when selected, will only search for values that match the case of the entry in the *Find what* field.

Match entire cell contents, when selected, ensures that the cell contains the same value as in the *Find what* field.

Replacing Data

To replace data, click on the *Replace* tab of the *Find and Replace* dialog box. On that tab, you get a *Replace with* field that allows you to enter the data you want to insert in place of what you find.

Then you get two additional buttons at the bottom of the screen:

Replace All – Automatically replaces all instances of the Find results.

Replace – Replace only the next one found.

All the other options on the screen remain the same on this tab.

Choose the range of values a cell will allow

Different minimums and maximums can be set for each cell. This process will also allow you to see if the cell you are working on will then affect other cells based on your current actions. Choose the cell you wish to add minimums or maximums to.

Select the menu labeled Data before selecting the option labeled Validation and choosing the tab labeled Settings.

Select the list labeled Allow and choose the option for whole numbers.

Choose the option labeled Data and then select Between.

Enter a minimum and a maximum number or a set of reference cells depending on your needs, and click on OK to ensure your specifics are saved.

Validate a cell based on the contents of another cell

Cells can also be set to only allow certain values based on their relationship to other cells.

Select the menu labeled Data before selecting the option labeled Validation and choosing the tab labeled Settings.

Choose the list labeled Allow, and the option labeled Customize.

Select the formula box and add the following to it: =IF(cell1>cell2, TRUE, FALSE) where cell1 and cell2 are the cells you wish to relate to one another. This formula can be used with any function, not just IF; it must always contain the equal sign as well as the true and false evaluation.

Select OK to save your function.

Allow a set of entries to be entered into a cell

To ensure a specific set of values are the only values that a specific cell or set of cells will accept, you must first create an acceptable list of values before setting the cell to only accept those values. The steps for doing so are outlined below:

Begin by clicking on cell A1 to select it

Go to the menu labeled Data before choosing the option for Validation

Select the option for settings, then choose the list option from the dropdown menu.

Find the box labeled source, and fill it in with a,b,c before selecting the OK option. This box can also be filled with a range that has been named or a specific reference to a cell that contains a set of values listed. If you chose this option, enter = before entering the specifics.

When done correctly, A1 will now show a list that provides a list of acceptable values. What you select will then appear in the cell. Values can also be typed into the cell though only allowed numbers will be allowed to remain.

Working With Cells And Ranges

Selecting Many Cells at one time

As we have already seen, If you want to select a cell, just click on the cell, and it is selected.

If you want to highlight many cells once, there is an approach to it. In that case, you are not selecting only one cell. An approach I use in selecting cells is the one I call *Clicking and Dragging*.

First, click the cell you want to start from

Position your pointer in the middle of the cell. Hold down your mouse button. Drag your pointer over all the cells you want to select

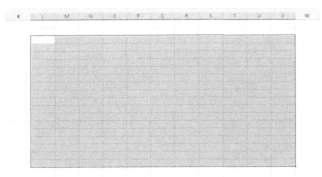

Release your mouse button

When the cells are selected, you will notice that the background color of the first cell is still white. That does not mean that the cell is not selected. It is just how Excel work.

Alternatively, you can click on the top-left cell in the range you want to select, for example, A3. While holding down the *Shift* key, click on the range's bottom-right cell, for example, E18.

This will select the range A3:E18.

Deselecting Cells

Sometimes when you're selecting several cells or ranges, you might accidentally select more cells than you intended. You can deselect any extra cells within the selected range with the deselect feature. To deselect cells within a selection, hold down the *CTRL* key, then click or click-and-drag to deselect any cells or ranges within the selection.

If you need to reselect any of the cells, hold down the *CTRL* key and click on the cells to select them again.

Note: This is a new feature starting from Excel 2019.

Cell Range

A Cell range is an identified group of cells. The use of a colon (:) between cell references determined a range. For example, A1:C1 is a range in a row, and it states that the cells included between A1 to C1 are selected, and all data in these cells will obey the same command.

◢	A	B	C	D
1				
2				=A1:C1
3				

Adding and deleting cells in Excel worksheet

Adding and deleting individual cells is an option when you are working on an Excel worksheet. Adding a new cell gives you the option to move the existing cells to the right or down. Deleting a cell gives you the option to move the existing cells to the left or up.

Add cells horizontally.

Select the cell that will be to the right of the new cell, and right-click with your mouse.

From the dropdown menu that appears, select *Insert,* and this will bring you a dialog box from which you will select *Shift cells right*, then click ok.

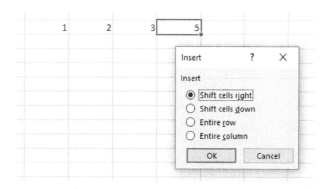

In the upper example, it will appear a new empty cell will be between the numbers 3 and 5.

Alternatively, you can use the *Insert* button in the *Cells* group in the *Home* tab.

Delete cells horizontally.

To delete a cell, do the same process. Select the one you want to delete, and instead of selecting *Insert* from the dropdown menu, select *Delete*.

Select *Shift cells left* and click *OK*

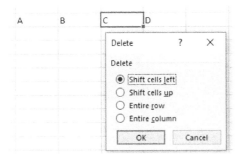

You will see the cell to the right of the deleted cell moving to its left.

Alternatively, to delete cells with the same process, you can use the *Delete* button inside the *Cells* group in the *Home* tab.

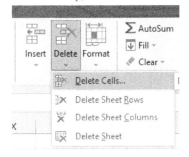

Add and Delete cells vertically

Adding and deleting cells vertically is the same process for those horizontal.

When you add a cell, choose the cell below where you wish the new cell to be placed, and then select *Shift cells down* in the *Insert* dialog box.

When you want to delete a cell, you will need to select it and then select *Shift cells up* in the *Insert* dialog box.

Naming cells

Naming a cell or range of cells makes it easier to understand and maintain that data and easier to remember if you may want to refer to it later, in a formula or another worksheet.

So to define a name of a cell, just select it, go to the *Name box* (at the left of the *Formula bar*), click on it, type the name you prefer, and *Enter* key.

In the example below, I have named the cell B2 "Oranges."

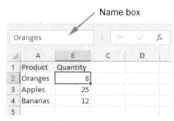

Name box

Now that your cell has a name, you can use it as a reference. If you want to recall a named cell wherever in your workbook, just type the sing "=" and the name that you gave the cell (when you start typing, it will appear automatically). Press *Enter* key, and the data from the cell will appear.

Let's recall the cell "Oranges" in cell D2. Here below, you can see the result.

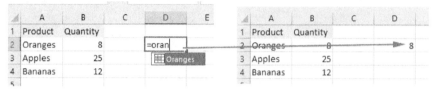

Add a name in the Name Box and save it by pressing the ENTER key.

The remaining characters can be underscores, periods, numbers, and letters. Excel will not distinguish capital and lowercase letters. If you wish to make the name, and therefore the cell or group of cells visible to the current workbook as a whole, add the prefix *Sheet1!* to the start of the name where Sheet1 is the sheet you are basing the data in.

You can also select the group of cells you wish to name, right-click and either choose a name yourself with the Define Name option or let Excel label the data for you with the *Pick From Drop Down List* option.

Additional naming options can be found on the Formulas tab under the Defined Names Sections.

Add Comments to Excel cells

In order to add a comment to one of your cells, just right-click on it and click on *Insert comment*.

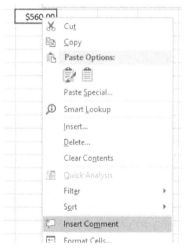

It will display a yellow box where you can type your comment. When finished, click outside the comment box. You will note a red triangle at the upper right corner indicating that the cell has a comment

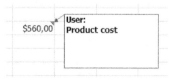

By selecting the cell, the comment will show up. You can then choose to edit, delete, or hide your comment. Simply right-click in the cell and select the command.

To display all the comments you have, go to the *Review* tab and click *Show All Comments* in the *Comments* Group. All the comments in the workbook will be displayed.

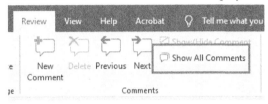

Working With Rows And Columns

As we already saw, columns run vertically across the worksheet. They are cells arranged in vertical order, and they range from A to XFD. Excel platforms make use of columns and rows to display information.

A row is a horizontal section across the spreadsheet which contains many cells, and they are labeled using Numbers (1, 2,3, and so on).

Insert a new column and row

Go to the *Home* tab and click the *Insert button* (Cells group).

For example, let's say you have data in columns A, B, C, and D, and you wish to insert a new column between C and D.

Click the column letter directly to the right of where you want to place the new column on the left. In our case will be column D. You will see it appear as a little black arrow by doing this.

	A	B	C	D
1	500	120	330	30
2	330	270	180	50
3	180	490	230	70
4	230	110	220	90
5				

Now right-click on the selected column and then select *Insert* from the pop-up menu.

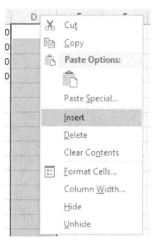

This will insert a new column between C and D. The data contained in column D will should be moved to column E. See below the before and after scenario.

	A	B	C	D
1	500	120	330	30
2	330	270	180	50
3	180	490	230	70
4	230	110	220	90

	A	B	C	D	E
1	500	120	330		30
2	330	270	180		50
3	180	490	230		70
4	230	110	220		90

To insert a new row, proceed in the same way. Click on the row number to select the whole row. Right-click and select *Insert* from the popup menu. This will insert a new row directly above the selected row.

See the example below where I have inserted a new row between rows 3 and 4.

	A	B	C	D
1	500	120	330	30
2	330	270	180	50
3	180	490	230	70
4	230	110	220	90
5				
6				

	A	B	C	D
1	500	120	330	30
2	330	270	180	50
3	180	490	230	70
4				
5	230	110	220	90
6				

You could also insert new rows and columns by using the *Insert* command button on the *Home* tab in the Cells group.

Note: By pressing the F4 key, you will repeat the last thing you did, so by pressing it, you are allowed to insert more than one row or column very quickly.

Inserting multiple rows or columns at the same time
Now you may be familiar already with how to insert a single row or column, so this will be quite easy.

Drag down the number of rows you want to insert by left-clicking on the row number just below where you want to place the additional rows. In the example below, I want to create 3 additional rows, so I clicked and dragged from row 3 to row 5 (3 rows in total).

	A	B	C	D
1	500	120	330	30
2	330	270	180	50
3	180	490	230	70
4	230	110	220	90
5	270	180	456	360
6	185	454	788	549
7	323	834	197	195
8				

Now just right-click on any of the selected rows and select *Insert*.

	A	B	C	D
1	500	120	330	30
2	330	270	180	50
3				
4				
5				
6	180	490	230	70
7	230	110	220	90
8	270	180	456	360
9	185	454	788	549
10	323	834	197	195

This will insert new rows above the row selected; in our example, 3 new rows above row number 3.

How to Extend Columns and Rows of a Cell

When you start making use of the excel application, you will find out that at a point, the words you type in a cell cut into the column of another cell. Let's have a look at how to adjust both columns and rows.

Let's say that we want to extend column A in the example below because the phrase inside cell A1 has been cut off when column B start.

	A	B	C
1	this is a fa	$1.986,00	
2			
3			

Click the column A heading, and position your cursor over the line between headings A and B.

	A	B	C
1	this is a fa	$1.986,00	
2			
3			
4			

Press down the left button of your mouse, and drag to the right to widen the column.

	A	B	C
1	this is a fantastic product	$1.986,00	
2			
3			

As you can see, column A has been extended, and the phrase "this is a fantastic product" is now completely discovered

To extend any row in your spreadsheet, just do the same process. Position your cursor over the line in the row heading, hold down the left button of your mouse and drag up or down to increase or decrease the row height.

In the example below, I have increased the row 1 height.

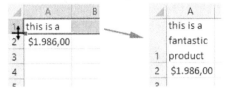

Turn rows into columns

Assume you have a dataset similar to the first one here below. The years are sorted in columns, and product names are sorted in rows. Let's convert columns to rows to transform the first graphic into the second one.

Select now all the data.

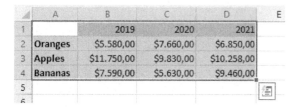

Copy the chosen cells by right-clicking on them and selecting *Copy* from the dialog box or by pressing CTRL+C.

Note: Choose now the destination range's first cell, making sure to choose a cell that is not in the same range as your original data so that the copy and paste portions do not overlap. For instance, if your existing datasheet has four 3 columns and 16 rows, the converted datasheet will have 16 columns and 3 rows.

Right-click on the destination cell, then pick *Paste Special*. From the *Paste Special* dialog box, select *Transpose* and click OK.

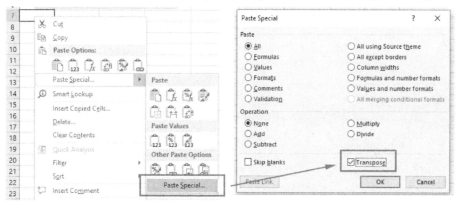

Note: this method has two limitations that prohibit it from being considered a complete solution for data transposition in Excel (come back here once you have read Modules C and D, which explain Tables and Formulas):

- It is not suitable for complete rotate Excel tables. If you copy the whole table and then open the *Paste Special* dialog, the *Transpose* option will be disabled. In this scenario, you must either replicate the table without the column headings or first convert it to a range.

- Because *Paste Special* > *Transpose* does not connect the new table to the source data, it is best suited for one-time conversions. You'd have to repeat the operation and rotate the table every time the source data changed. No one wants to spend time translating the same rows and columns again and over, right?

How to delete Blank Rows

Having blank rows might cause a document to take up much more space than required.

Let's use the *Find and Select* command to fix this issue, so select it from the *Editing* group on the *Home* tab.

From the dropdown menu, click *Go To Special…*, select *Blanks*, and click *OK*. The blank cells are now selected by Excel.

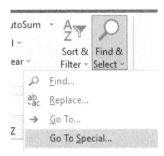

Note: After that, Excel will highlight all of the blank cells. Make sure that just the cells you wish to deleted are highlighted before to proceed. If you just want to eliminate rows rather than individual blank cells, you may always deselect a cell by pressing CTRL+Click. Remember that when you remove a cell, the underlying data moves higher.

	A	B	C	D	E
1		2019	2020	2021	
2	Oranges	$5.580,00	$7.660,00	$6.850,00	
3	Apples	$11.750,00	$9.830,00	$10.258,00	
4					
5	Bananas	$7.590,00	$5.630,00	$9.460,00	
6					
7	Peaches	$6.480,00	$5.980,00	$9.420,00	
8	Pears	$3.600,00	$4.680,00	$4.120,00	
9					

Click now *Delete* from the *Cells* group on the *Home* tab, and the job is done.

	A	B	C	D
1		2019	2020	2021
2	Oranges	$5.580,00	$7.660,00	$6.850,00
3	Apples	$11.750,00	$9.830,00	$10.258,00
4	Bananas	$7.590,00	$5.630,00	$9.460,00
5	Peaches	$6.480,00	$5.980,00	$9.420,00
6	Pears	$3.600,00	$4.680,00	$4.120,00

Working With The Worksheets

Add a worksheet
Choose the sum icon, which means add (+) below on the screen displayed. Or, you can click on the *Home* tab, then go on Insert and then choose the option of Add Sheet.

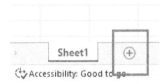

Renaming the worksheet
Click twice on the name of the sheet and easily change the name. Or, you can click on the *Sheet tab* with the right-click, select *Rename* option from the popup box, and write a new one.

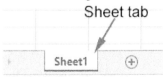

Delete a worksheet
You can right-click on the *Sheet* tab and then select *Delete*. Or, select the Sheet, go to the *Home* tab, select the *Delete* option, and click on *Delete Sheet*.

Moving Worksheets Between Workbooks

Move or Copy

Open the source workbook, which includes the worksheets to be moved or copied, and the destination workbook, which will contain the worksheets. To copy or transfer worksheets between them, you have to first open both the source and destination.

Use the *Arrange All* command, in the *View* tab to arrange the windows side-by-side.

To activate the workbook containing the worksheets that need to be relocated or duplicated, click on it.

Click again, at the bottom of the screen, on the sheet tab to pick it (hold down the *CTRL* key in order to select more than one worksheet at the same time).

Click on the *Format* button (*Home* tab) and select *Move or Copy Sheet…* from the menu, and a toolbox will appear

Select now the destination workbook in the *To Book* field. In the *Before sheet* field, choose where you want the worksheet to be located inside the destination workbook.

Select the Create a copy checkbox to make a copy of the worksheet rather than moving it.

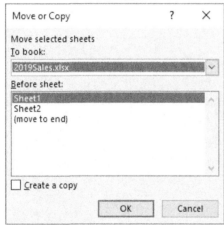

To finish the transfer or copy operation and exit the dialog box, click OK.

Drag and Drop

You can also use drag-and-drop, as you do it for data, to move worksheets between workbooks.

To do it in this way, arrange the workbooks side-by-side on the screen so that you can view both by using the *Arrange All* command, as mentioned above. Ideally, they should be arranged vertically.

Select the worksheet to be relocated or duplicated by clicking on the sheet tab in the destination workbook.

With your mouse, drag the sheet from the original worksheet to the destination workbook. The sheet you're transferring will be represented by a little document icon.

To copy the sheet (rather than move it), hold down the *CTRL key* while dragging it from the source worksheet to the destination workbook. If you're copying the sheet, the document icon will contain a plus sign (+).

How to Cover and Uncover a Worksheet

When you cover or hide worksheets, the data in them are also hidden. But you can uncover or unhide any worksheet at any time.

Let's see how to hide a worksheet. Go on the tab of the sheet you want to hide or cover and right-click on it. Click on the Hide button to cover any worksheet.

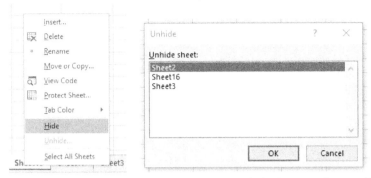

If you want to unhide any worksheets, right-click on any of your *Sheet* tabs, and select *Unhide…* Select from the pop box the sheet you want to Unhide, and it will appear again between the others worksheets.

Then, click the OK icon to set up the feature.

Note: if you want to hide multiple sheets, press down the CTRL key and select all the tabs of the Sheets that you wish to hide. Right-click on any sheet tab and select *Hide*.

MODULE B

CHAPTER 3: FORMATTING

Cells Formatting

By default, all cells content has the same formatting, making a workbook with a lot of information difficult to read. Basic formatting will help you design the texture of your workbook, allowing you to highlight particular sections and making your content easier to understand and view.

You can create defined and clear boundaries for different segments of your worksheet using cell borders and fill colors. To further distinguish our header cells from the rest of the worksheet, we'll add cell borders and fill color to them.

Apply Borders

Begin by highlighting the cells to which you wish to apply your borders. Then, locate the *Borders* dropdown menu in the *Font* tab, and choose one of the pre-installed designs. It's very intuitive; see here below for some examples.

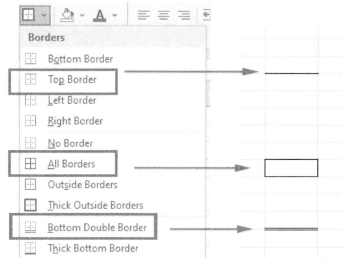

The *Format Cells* dialog box is another option for adding borders to cells. While it includes many of the same border-applying capabilities, it also gives you access to a lot of extra possibilities.

To proceed in this way, select the cell you would like to format and right-click on it.

Then from the drop-down menu, select *Format Cells.*

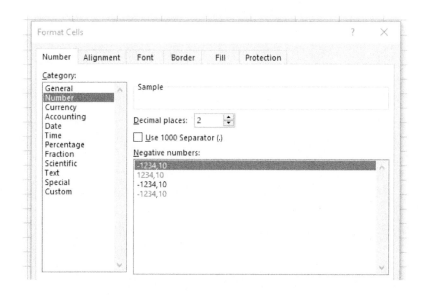

Here you have all the below tabs to format cells and data:

- Number tab – specifies the numerical data form, such as dollar, date, or percentage.

- Alignment tab – helps you move and coordinate data inside a cell.

- Font tab – helps you modify cell font attributes such as font face, height, type, and color.

- Border – enables you to choose a border theme for your cell from a number of choices.

- Fill – helps you shade and paint the backdrop of a cell.

- Cell protection – the ability to secure or shield a cell.

Let's focus on the border tab. Here you can find a wide variety of border possibilities that you may play with. We choose the following options for our example below:

- A dashed line Style (#1) for the Outline Presets (#3).

- A double line Style (#5) for the Inside Presets (#4).

- A dark grey color (#2) for all the borders.

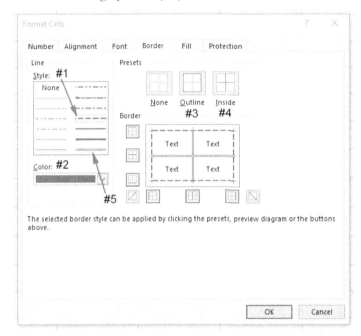

When you've finished setting all of your border options, click OK to close the dialog box. Your borders will now be applied to your chosen cells.

Note: As you can apply a border to one cell, you can do it for a range of selected cells. In the picture above, you can see the range of cells selected and what has become after applying the border's style.

Fill a Cell with Colour

To add color to the backdrop of your cell, first, pick it by clicking on it. Click on the arrow to the right of the *Fill Color* icon, then pick the color from the drop-down menu. The backdrop color will be changed to the color you choose.

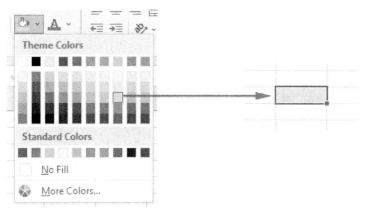

By selecting a range of cells, the chosen color will be applied to all of them as for the borders.

Clearing the Cell Format

To remove formatting from a cell or range, do the following:

Select the cells you want to clear.

Select *Home* and click *Clear* (from the *Editing* group).

A pop-up menu with several options will be displayed (Clear All, Clear Formats, Clear Contents, Clear Comments, and Clear Hyperlinks)

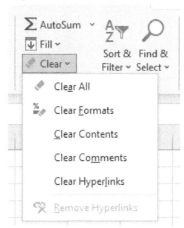

To clear just the format and not the values, click on *Clear Formats.*

This will return the format of the selected cells to *General,* which is the Excel default.

Font

Font Style

You can alter your font style by selecting (highlighting) the data and clicking on the font pane to select the style you wish to use for the input data. Excel comes with a variety of good-looking fonts varying from Calibri to Arial to Verdana and so on.

Font size

Choose the cells you need to modify.

The chosen font size will be applied to the text.

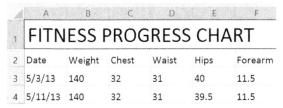

You can also use your keyboard to enter a customized font size or use the Increase and Decrease Font Size controls. If you click the bigger *A*, it will increase your font size, and if you click the smaller *A*, it will decrease the font size.

Every new workbook's font is set to Calibri by default. However, Excel has a variety of fonts that you can use to modify your cell text.

Choose the cells you want to update.

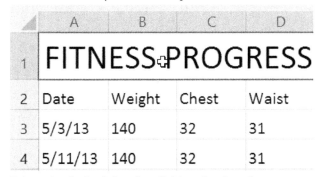

Select the desired font by clicking the dropdown arrow next to the Font command on the *Home* tab.

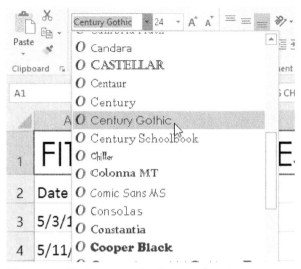

The text will change to the font you've chosen.

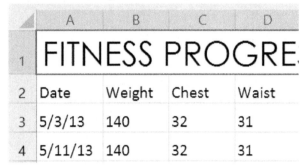

When composing a workbook at the workplace, choose a font that is easy to read. Standard reading fonts include Times New Roman, Cambria, Calibri, and Arial.

Font Color

To modify the color of your data, click the colored pane beneath the typeface tab; this will provide a drop-down menu of color possibilities from which to pick (see below how it appear)

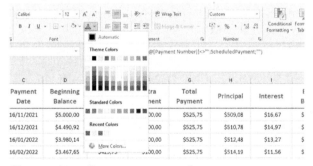

Choose the cells you want to update.

Select the desired font color by clicking the dropdown arrow next to the Font Color command on the *Home* tab.

The text will change to the font color you've chosen.

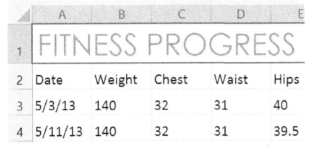

To see more color options, go to the bottom of the menu and choose More Colors.

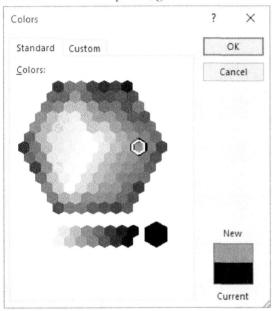

Bold, Italics, and Underline

To add either bold, italics, underline, or any combination of any of them, first highlight the data you wish to format, navigate to the font pane under the home tab, and select your desired format option. If you wish to apply:

- bold format, click on the *B* icon,

- underline format, click the *U* icon,

- italics format, click the *I* icon.

In case you wish to apply more than one of these format options, just click the combination you want to use.

Choose the cells you decide to modify.

On the *Home* tab, select the Italic, Bold, or Underline (U) command. I use the bold command in the example below.

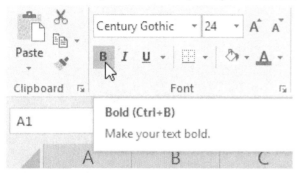

The text will be styled in the chosen format.

	A	B	C	D	E
1	FITNESS PROGRESS				
2	Date	Weight	Chest	Waist	Hips
3	5/3/13	140	32	31	40
4	5/11/13	140	32	31	39.5

You can also make selected text italicized by pressing CTRL +I, bold by pressing CTRL +B, and underlined by pressing CTRL +U on your keyboard.

Formatting Data into Table

There are times when you will have a range of data that you would love to format into a table. To do this, select the range of data you wish to format into a table

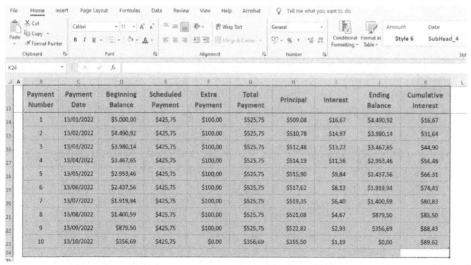

Now navigate to the *format as table* in the style pane in the *Home* tab. A drop-down will show indicating different table formats; choose the one that best suits your data.

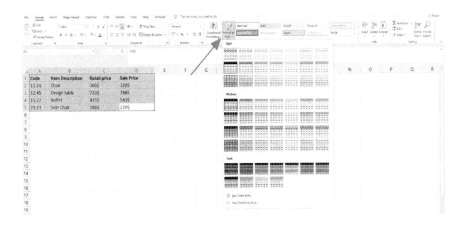

Once you select the table format, immediately a pop-up will show up requesting your confirmation of the cell involved. Click ok to proceed and your data will be transformed into a table form, as shown below.

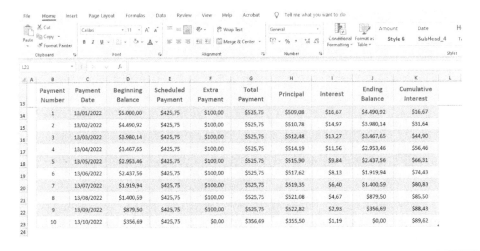

Number Formats

It's a good idea to use suitable number formats for your data while you're working with a spreadsheet. Number formats stipulate what kind of specifics you're using in your spreadsheet, such as currency ($), percentages (%), dates, times, zip code, phone number, and so on. Number formats make the spreadsheet easier to read and use. When you add a number format to a cell, you're telling your spreadsheet what kind of values are stored there. The date format, for example, tells the spreadsheet that you're entering particular calendar dates. This helps the spreadsheet to effectively represent your data, ensuring that your data is accurate and your formulas are measured correctly. If you don't specify a number format, the spreadsheet will most likely use the general number format by default. The general format, on the other hand, can make minor formatting changes to your data.

Applying number formats

Number formats are applied in the same way as other forms of formatting, such as changing the font color by selecting cells and selecting the desired formatting option. There are two methods for selecting a number format: On the *Home* tab, select the required format from the Number Format drop-down menu in the Number group. You can also use one of the convenient number-formatting commands displayed below the drop-down menu.

To access more number-formatting options, select required cells and press CTRL+1 on your keyboard.

We've used the Currency number format in this example, which introduces currency symbols ($) and shows two decimal places for any quantitative values.

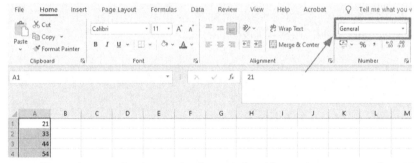

You will see the actual value in the formula bar if you choose any cells with number formatting. This value will be used in formulas and other calculations in the spreadsheet.

On the *Home* tab, locate the Number group and click the drop-down list to display a number of formats.

The selected cell/range will now be formatted in the format you selected.

Accessing *More Number Formats…* will let you choose a format that is not on the drop-down list;

Let's have a look at how to use it. For example, if you're in the US and you want to change the currency from US dollars to UK pounds:

At the bottom of the drop-down list, select *More Number Formats…* at the bottom of the drop-down list (shown above) or click on the dialog box launcher (the small diagonal arrow at the bottom-right of the Number group).

The Format Cells window will be displayed.

Click on the Symbol field to display a drop-down list. Select the British pound sign (£) from the list.

On this screen, you can also set the number of decimal places and the format you want for negative numbers. The Sample field gives you a preview of how the chosen format will look on your worksheet.

Click OK to confirm your changes when done.

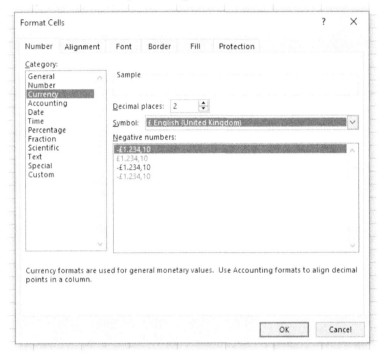

Creating Custom Numeric Formats

If none of the existing formats fit your needs, you can design your own unique format.

Assume you have a column in your worksheet where you keep track of a set of numbers. Unique product IDs, product serial numbers, or phone numbers. You may prefer that the numbers be displayed in a certain format regardless of how they were entered.

In Excel, you can define your own format for a set of cells so that every data is formatted with your preferred format. To create your own format:

Right-click any area in your selection and choose *Format Cells* from the pop-up menu. Alternatively, launch the *Format Cells* window by clicking the dialog box launcher in the *Number* group on the *Home* tab.

Under Category, select Custom.

In the Type box, select an existing format close to the one you would like to create.

Note: If you find a format on the list that meets your needs, then you can just select that one and click OK.

In the Type box, type in the format you want to create. For example, 0000-00000.

Click OK.

In the image above, column A has a set of numbers. Column B shows the same numbers with a custom format (0000-0000000) now applied to them.

Using number formats correctly

Number formatting involves more than just selecting cells and adding a format. Based on how you enter data, spreadsheets will automatically add number formatting. This means you'll need to enter data in a format that the program understands and then double-check that the numbers in those cells are formatted correctly. For example, the image below demonstrates how to properly format dates, times, and percentages using number formats.

Percentage formats

The percentage (%) format is one of the most useful number formats. Values are shown as percentages, such as 15% or 65%. This is particularly useful when estimating data like sales tax or a tip. The percentage number format is added to that specific cell automatically when you type a percent sign (%) after a number.

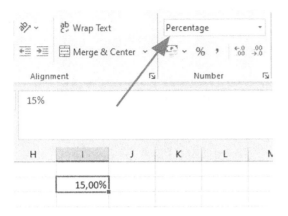

Percentage formatting can be helpful in different situations. For example, note how the sales tax rate is configured differently for each spreadsheet (5, 5%, and 0.05) in the picture below:

No percentage formatting   Percentage formatting   Written as decimal

The estimation in the spreadsheet on the left didn't seem to fit correctly, as you can see. Our spreadsheet assumes we want to multiply $22.50 by 5 instead of 5% if we don't use the percentage number format. Although the spreadsheet on the right is still functional without percentage formatting, the spreadsheet in the center is more understandable.

Date formats

When dealing with dates, use a date format to show that you're referring to particular calendar dates, such as June 25, 2014. Date formats also give you access to a useful set of date functions that calculate an answer using time and date information.

Spreadsheets do not perceive information in the same way as humans do. For example, if you type July into a cell, the spreadsheet will not consider it as a date and treat it like any other text. So, you'll need to insert dates in a format that your spreadsheet understands, such as day/month/year or month/day/year. We'll type 10/12/2014 for October 12, 2014, in the example below. The date number format for the cell will be implemented automatically by our spreadsheet.

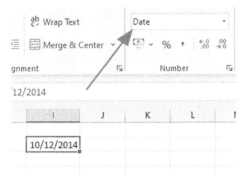

Now that we've formatted our data correctly, we can use it for a variety of purposes.

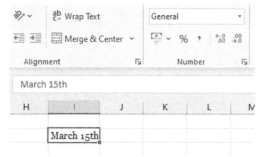

Since the spreadsheet didn't understand that we were referring to a date, this cell is still formatted as a number.

When we type March 15 (without the "th"), the spreadsheet acknowledges it as a date. Due to the absence of a year, the spreadsheet would automatically add the current year, ensuring that the data contains all the required details. The date could be typed in a variety of forms, like 3/15/2014, 3/15, or March 15, 2014, and the spreadsheet will acknowledge it as a date.

Try entering the following dates into a spreadsheet to determine if the date format is automatically implemented.

- October 2014
- October 12, 2017
- 10/6/2015
- 10/11

- October
- October 14
- October 12th

Other date formatting options

Select More Number Formats from the Number Format drop-down menu to see more date formatting options. There are options for displaying the date in a certain way, such as adding the day or ignoring the year.

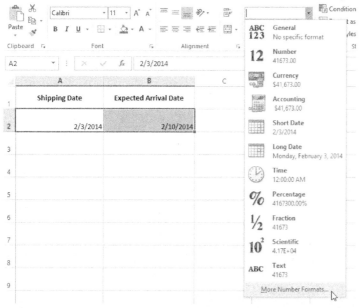

A dialog box called Format Cells will appear.

You can select the required date formatting option from this menu.

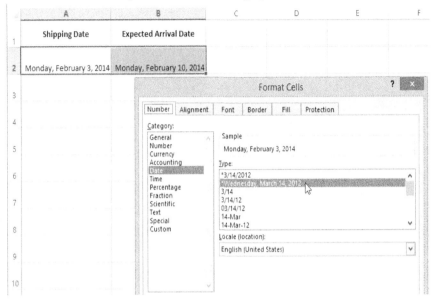

A custom date format doesn't change the date in our cell; it only changes how it's displayed, as you can see in the formula bar.

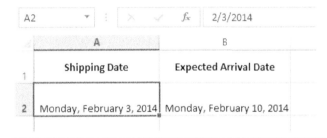

The10 Best Commands For Data Formatting

Copy Cell Formatting

A quick way to format a cell or group of cells based on another cell is to use the *Format Painter*. This can be found in the *Clipboard* group on the *Home* tab. This can save a lot of time as you only create the format once and copy it to other cells in your worksheet for which you would like to apply that format.

To copy cell formatting with the Format Painter:

Click on the source cell; that is the cell you want to copy the format from.

Select *Home* and click the *Format Painter*.

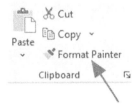

Click and drag over the destination cells, i.e., the cells you want to copy the format to. The destination cells will now have the same format as the source cell.

Example: If cell A2 is formatted as *Currency* and you want to format A3 to A14 as currency with the *Format Painter*, you would carry out the following steps:

Click on cell A2 to select it.

Click on Format Painter.

Select A3 to A14, and the job is done.

The currency format from A2 will now be applied to A3:A14.

Text and Cell Alignments

There are three horizontal alignment options: against the left, against the right, and in the center. There are three vertical alignment options as well: against the top border, against the bottom border, and in the center.

To modify the text alignment in Excel, select the cell(s) to be realigned, navigate to the *Home* tab > Alignment group, and pick the appropriate option:

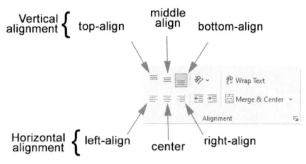

- Vertical Alignment. To align data vertically, choose one of the following icons:

- Top Align. - aligns the contents of the cell to the top.

- Middle Align. - centers the contents of the cell between the top and bottom.

- Bottom Alignment Bottom Align. - aligns the contents to the cell's bottom.

- Horizontal Alignment. Microsoft Excel gives the following options for horizontally aligning your data:

- Align Left - aligns the contents of the cell along the left edge.

- Center - places the items in the cell's center.

- Align Right - aligns the contents of the cell along the right edge.

Indent

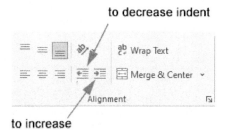

The Tab key in Microsoft Excel does not indent text in a cell as it does in Microsoft Word; it just transfers the cursor to the next cell. Use the Indent icons located just under the Orientation button to modify the indentation of the cell contents.

Click the Increase Indent button to move the text to the right. If you've gone too far to the right, click the Decrease Indent button to return the text to the left.

Wrap Text

When the data entered in a cell is too big to fit, one of two things happens:

If any of the columns to the right are empty, a lengthy text string stretches over the cell boundary into those columns.

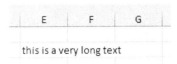

If the right column it's filled with some data, your text will be hidden as you can see below.

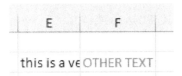

Wrapping text in a cell makes it easier to view all the data in that cell. The term "wrapping text" refers to showing the contents of a cell on more than one line rather than one long line.

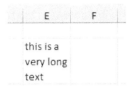

To use the *Wrap Text* command in excel, take these steps:

1. Select the cell containing the text you want to format in worksheet.

2. Click on the *Wrap Text* command at the *Home* tab. You can as well select the cell and press the shortcut Alt + H + W.

Merge and center

The cells merge style tool is used to merge different cells in the worksheet as one.

The *Merge and Center* option is the quickest and simplest method to integrate two or more cells.

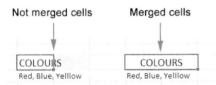

This is the easy two steps procedure:

Choose the adjacent cells that you wish to merge.

Click the Merge & Center button on the *Home* tab > Alignment group.

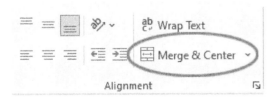

Applying Cell Styles

To format a cell or range with a different style:

- Select the cell or range.

- Select Home > Styles.

- You can mouse over the different styles to get a preview on your worksheet before you select one.

- Select a style from the pop-up menu.

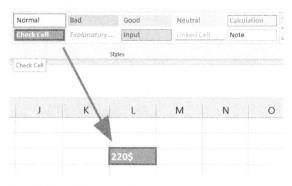

Conditional Formatting

With conditional formatting, you can format your data based on certain conditions to display a visual representation that helps you spot critical issues and identify patterns and trends. For example, you can use visual representations to clearly show the highs and lows in your data and the trend based on a set of criteria.

In the example below, we can quickly see the trend in sales and how they compare to each other.

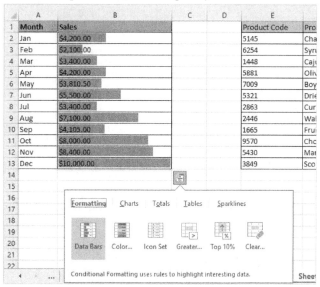

To quickly apply a conditional format:

- Select the range of cells you wish to format. The quick analysis button will be displayed at the bottom-right of the selection.

- Click the Quick Analysis button, and use the default *Formatting* tab.

- When you mouse over the formatting options, you'll see a live preview of what your data will look like when applied.

- Click on *Data Bars* (or any of the other options) to apply the formatting to your data.

Use Multiple Conditional Formats

You may use multiple conditional formats on the same group of cells.

To do so, select the cells, click the Quick Analysis button, and click another format option, for example, Icon Set.

The arrows are used to depict the upper, middle, and lower values in the set of data.

Formatting Text Fields

For example, if we wanted to highlight all the rows with "Sauce" in the name, we would:

Select the range. Click the Quick Analysis button.

Select *Text…* from the Formatting options.

In the *Text That Contains* dialog, we would enter **Sauce** in the first box and select the type of formatting we want from the drop-down list.

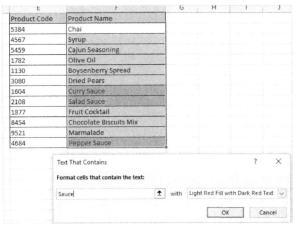

You can explore the formatting options for different data types by selecting the data to be formatted and clicking on the *Quick Analysis* button.

Creating Conditional Formatting Rules

An alternative way to create conditional formatting is by creating Rules in Excel.

To launch the *New Formatting Rule* dialog:

On the Ribbon, click on Home > Conditional Formatting > New Rule.

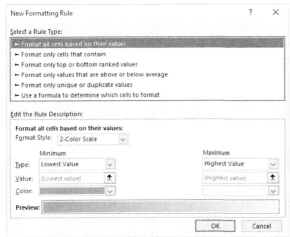

You can use this dialog to create more complex rules using a series of conditions and criteria.

You can select a rule type from the following options:

Format all cells based on their values.

Format only cells that contain.

Format only top or bottom-ranked values.

For each rule type, the bottom half of the screen, labeled *Edit the Rule Description*, gives you different fields to define your rule.

Example:

Let's say you had a products table and you wanted to format the whole row grey if the product stock fell below 10.

To do this, you select the range you want to conditionally format, i.e., A2:C18. Note that A2 is the active cell.

On the *Ribbon*, you click Conditional Formatting > New Rule and select Use a formula to determine which cells to format.

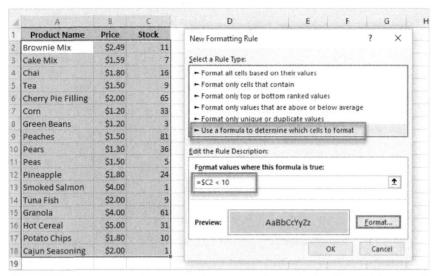

Since A2 is the active cell, you need to enter a formula that is valid for row 2 and will apply to all the other rows.

To do this, you type in the formula =$C2 < 10. The dollar sign before the C means it is an *absolute reference* for column C ($C). With this, the value in column C for each row is evaluated and used for the conditional formatting.

For the fill color, click the *Format* button, select the fill color you want and click OK and OK again to apply the rule.

The rows with Stock below 10 will now be filled with grey.

Carrying out Calculations with Formulas

Excel provides tools and features that enable you to carry out different types of calculations, from basic arithmetic to complex engineering calculations using functions.

Conditionally Formatting Time

Let's say we had a task list, and we wanted to see which ones were late, **i.e.,** the ones with the due date before today.

You have to select the cells in the *Due date* column.

Click the *Quick Analysis* button, and then click *Less Than*.

Type in =TODAY()

We could type in today's date, but that would mean we would need to update the conditional formatting daily, and that could get tedious fast! The TODAY function will always return today's date.

Select the formatting you'd like to use from the dropdown list.

Click *OK*.

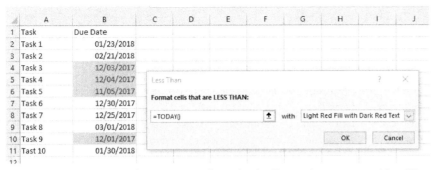

The tasks that are overdue now stand out in the list and are easy to identify at a glance.

CHAPTER 4: EXCEL ESSENTIAL FEATURES

Paste Special

One of the more popular Excel tasks is grabbing (or copying) data from one cell and pasting it into another. However, there is a lot you might want to copy (formatting, value, algorithm, notes, and so on), and you might not want to copy anything. The most popular scenario is where you try to remove the markup and save the data to your own spreadsheet using your own formatting. Frequently, one will want to convert the elements in a data row or into a column. Copying and pasting each individual header will take a long time. Not to mention that one might potentially fall victim to one of the most common and costly Excel pitfalls: human failure. Enable Excel to do the heavy lifting for you. Go ahead and choose the column or row that one wants to transfer. Copy by right-clicking and selecting "Copy." Then, in the spreadsheet, pick the cells where one wants the first row or column to start. After right-clicking on the cell, choose Paste Special from the context menu. Select the choice to translate when the module appears.

Paste Special is one of those functions that people use over and over again. One may also opt to copy formulas, formats, even column widths or values in the module. This is particularly useful when copying the results of the pivot table into a structured and graphed chart.

Remove The Formula But Keep The Result (Forse Da Mettere Nel Capitolo Delle Formule)

When one removes the formula by pushing the Delete key, it also deletes a measured value. You should, however, remove just the formula and leave the outcome in the cell. Here's how to do it:

For the formulas, choose all cells.

To duplicate the selected cells, press CTRL + C.

To paste the computed values back into the chosen cells, right-click the selection and choose Paste Values from Values. Alternatively, click Shift+F10, then V to use the Paste Special shortcut.

Entering Data

Click on a cell in the worksheet area, and a rectangular box will appear around the cell. This is the *cell pointer* or the active cell.

To enter data, simply type it directly into the cell, or you can click on the formula bar and type the data in there.

Editing data: When typing in the worksheet area, if you want to make a correction use the *BACKSPACE* key to go back and not the left arrow key. The arrow keys move the cell pointer from cell to cell. To use the arrow keys when editing data, select the cell, then click on the formula bar to edit the data there.

To overwrite data, click in the cell to make it the active cell and just type in the new value. This will overwrite the previous value.

If you only want to edit parts of the data in a cell, for example, a piece of text, then select the cell and click on the formula bar to edit the contents there.

Deleting data: To delete data from your worksheet, select the data and hit the *Delete* key.

Default content alignment: In Excel, numbers and formulas are right-aligned in the cell by default. Everything else is left-aligned by default. So, you can tell if Excel recognizes your entry as a number or text value.

Date and Time

The date and time can be easily inserted into your excel workbook. Date and time changing in Excel do not require you to check the current date before inserting. When you press key combinations such as CTRL+, in order to insert the current date in a cell, excel does take a snapshot of the current date and then inserts the date in the cell because the cell value does not change. Select the cell where you want to insert the current date and time in the workbook. And follow the following steps:

Press CTRL+; (semi-colon) to insert the current date.

If you want to insert the current time, press CTRL;(semi-colon), then press CTRL+Shift+; (semi-colon).

Choose the range of values a cell will allow

Different minimums and maximums can be set for each cell. This process will also allow you to see if the cell you are working on will then affect other cells based on your current actions.

Choose the cell you wish to add minimums or maximums too.

Select the menu labeled Data before selecting the option labeled Validation and choosing the tab labeled Settings.

Select the list labeled Allow and choose the option for whole numbers.

Choose the option labeled Data and then select Between.

Enter a minimum and a maximum number or a set of reference cells depending on your needs, and click on OK to ensure your specifics are saved.

Validate a cell based on the contents of another cell

Cells can also be set to only allow certain values based on their relationship to other cells.

Select the menu labeled Data before selecting the option labeled Validation and choosing the tab labeled Settings.

Choose the list labeled Allow, and the option labeled Customize.

Select the formula box and add the following to it: =IF(cell1>cell2, TRUE, FALSE) where cell1 and cell2 are the cells you wish to relate to one another. This formula can be used with any function, not just IF; it must always contain the equal sign as well as the true and false evaluation.

Select OK to save your function.

Allow a set of entries to be entered into a cell

To ensure a specific set of values are the only values that a specific cell or set of cells will accept, you must first create an acceptable list of values before setting the cell to only accept those values. The steps for doing so are outlined below:

Begin by clicking on cell A1 to select it

Go to the menu labeled Data before choosing the option for Validation

Select the option for settings, then choose the list option from the dropdown menu.

Find the box labeled source, and fill it in with a,b,c before selecting the OK option. This box can also be filled with a range that has been named or a specific reference to a cell that contains a set of values listed. If you chose this option, enter = before entering the specifics.

When done correctly, A1 will now show a list that provides a list of acceptable values. What you select will then appear in the cell. Values can also be typed into the cell though only allowed numbers will be allowed to remain.

Autofill

The Autofill feature in Excel enables you to fill cells with a series of sequential dates and numbers. It enables you to automate repetitive tasks as it is smart enough to figure out what data goes in a cell-based on another cell when you drag the fill handle across cells.

Entering Dates with AutoFill

You may have a worksheet where you need to enter dates. You can enter **January** in one cell and use the AutoFill feature to automatically enter the rest of the months.

To AutoFill dates, enter **January** or any other starting month in one cell, then grab the small fill handle and drag it across the other cells.

AutoFill also works with abbreviations, but they must be 3 letters. For example, if you enter Jan and then drag down, it will be filled with Feb, Mar, Apr, May, **etc.**

Let's say you want to enter the 7 days of the week as your row headings. In the first cell of your range, enter **Monday** or **Mon**. Then drag the autofill handle down over the remaining 6 cells. This will AutoFill the remaining cells from Tuesday to Sunday.

Excel keeps the filled days selected, giving you a chance to drag the handle back if you went too far or to drag it further if you didn't go far enough.

You can also use the *AutoFill Options* drop-down menu to further refine your fill options. To access the AutoFill options, with the cells still selected, you will see a drop-down button that appears on the last cell.

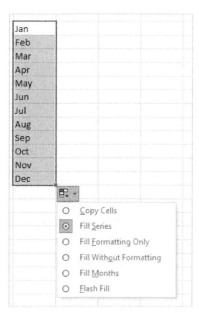

Note: If you don't see a button that enables you to access the AutoFill Options drop-down menu (shown above) after an autofill, it is most likely because the option hasn't been set in Excel Options.

To enable AutoFill Options (if it isn't available), navigate to:

File > Options > Advanced.

Under the *Cut, copy, and paste* section, select the checkbox for the *Show Paste Options* button when content is posted.

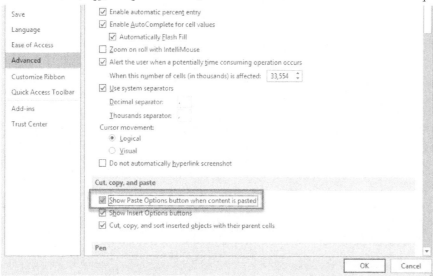

AutoFill Incremental Values

To AutoFill other incremental values, you need to first let Excel know what the difference is. So, you would need to enter values in at least two cells before dragging the fill handle across the other cells.

Let's say you want to enter dates that increment by seven days, i.e., a weekly interval. You would need to enter two dates (for example, 01/10/19 and 01/17/19). Then you select both cells and drag across the empty cells to autofill the other cells with dates having an interval of 7 days.

You can do the same with other numbers. If you enter 1 and then drag down, the number 1 will just be copied to the other cells. However, if you enter numbers 1 and 2 in two cells and then select both cells and drag them down, you will get 3, 4, 5, 6, etc.

AutoFill Formulas

If the cell references are relative, then the references will also change to match the position of the active cell.

Note: If the cell references in your formula are absolute, then the cell references will not change when you use AutoFill to copy it to other cells.

AutoFill the Same Values

To AutoFill the same value across a series of cells, enter the value in the first cell, then hold down the *CTRL* key while dragging the fill handle across the other cells.

For example, if you want to fill a range of cells with $6.99:

Enter *$6.99* in the first cell.

Hold down the CTRL key.

Move your mouse pointer to the bottom-right of the cell and grab the autofill handle (small square) and then drag it across the other cells.

If you always use the same list of separate worksheets, you might consider adding it to the AutoFill list; this can save you a lot of time in the future. Click the Custom List tab from the Tools, Options...menu after selecting the set. Select Import, then Well.

Sort And Filter

Sorting Data

Excel offers a wide array of methods to sort your data, from a quick and basic sort to more complex sorts using your own custom list. We will be covering the popular methods in this section.

Quick Sort

To quickly sort data in Excel, select any single cell in the column you want to sort.

Right-click the cell. From the pop-up menu, select *Sort A to Z* (for ascending) or *Sort Z to A* (for descending).

If your column is a number field, you'll have *Sort Smallest to Largest* (for ascending) or *Sort Largest to Smallest* (for descending).

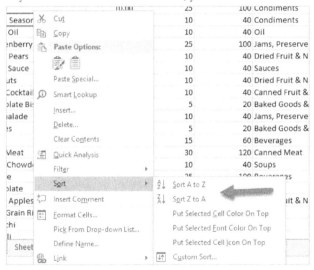

The sort does not change your data in any way. It simply reorders your rows according to the sort order and column you've chosen.

Custom Sort

In the example above, we sorted using just one column. However, you can sort using multiple columns; for example, in the data shown below, we may want to sort by <u>Category</u> and <u>Product name</u>. In this case, we would use the Custom Sort command on the *Ribbon*.

Applying a custom sort: Select a single cell anywhere in the data.

This will display the Sort dialog box.

In the *Sort On* the list, you have the option of selecting Values, Cell Color, Font Color, or Cell Icon. If you're sorting by value, you'll leave this as the default (Value).

In the *Order* list, select the order in which you want to sort. For a text column, you can choose *A to Z* (ascending order) or *Z to A* (descending order).

For a number column, you can choose *Smallest to Largest* or *Largest to Smallest*.

Click *OK* when you're done.

Sorting with a *Custom* List

When you click on the *Order* list, you can also select *Custom List* from the drop-down list and sort data by days of the week or months. You can add your own list (if the pre-defined ones do not meet your needs). This is useful when you want to sort using your own custom order rather than the standard ascending or descending order.

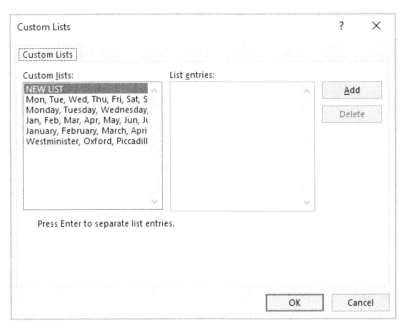

Filtering Data

Excel tables would have column headings by default; however, if your data is not an Excel table, ensure you have column headings like Category, Product Name, Price, etc. This makes using sort much easier.

	Category	Product Name	Price	Reorder Level	Target Level
2	Beverages	Chai	18.00	10	40
3	Condiments	Syrup	10.00	25	100
4	Condiments	Cajun Seasoning	22.00	10	40
5	Oil	Olive Oil	21.35	10	40
6	Jams, Preserves	Boysenberry Spread	25.00	25	100
7	Dried Fruit & Nuts	Dried Pears	30.00	10	40
8	Sauces	Curry Sauce	40.00	10	40

You can add column headings to your data by inserting a new row at the top of your worksheet and entering the headings. This is important because Excel will use the first row for the filter arrows.

How to filter data:

Select any cell within the data that you want to filter. Click on *Home > Sort & Filter > Filter* (or click *Data > Filter*). You will get a *filter arrow* at the top of each column. This is also called an *AutoFilter*. Note that in Excel tables, filter arrows are turned on by default.

Click the AutoFilter of the column you want to filter. For example, Price.

Uncheck *Select All* and check the values you want to use for the filter.

Click *OK*.

	A	B	C	D	E
1	Product Code	Product Name	Price	Reorder Level	Category
16	NWTSO-41	Clam Chowder	$9.65	10	Soups
17	NWTB-43	Coffee	$46.00	25	Beverages
18	NWTCA-48	Chocolate	$12.75	25	Candy
19	NWTDFN-51	Dried Apples	$53.00	10	Dried Fruit & Nuts
20	NWTG-52	Long Grain Rice	$7.00	25	Grains
21	NWTP-56	Gnocchi	$38.00	30	Pasta
22	NWTP-57	Ravioli	$19.50	20	Pasta
23	NWTS-65	Hot Pepper Sauce	$21.05	10	Sauces
24	NWTS-66	Tomato Sauce	$17.00	20	Sauces
25	NWTD-72	Mozzarella	$34.80	10	Dairy Products
26	NWTDFN-74	Almonds	$10.00	5	Dried Fruit & Nuts
27	NWTCO-77	Mustard	$13.00	15	Condiments
28	NWTDFN-80	Dried Plums	$3.50	50	Dried Fruit & Nuts
29	NWTB-81	Green Tea	$2.99	100	Beverages
30	NWTC-82	Granola	$4.00	20	Cereal

The AutoFilter changes to a funnel icon to show that the column is filtered. If you look at the row heading numbers, you'll see that they're now blue, indicating which rows are included in the filtered data.

Applying a Custom Filter

Click on the AutoFilter of the column you want to use for the filter.

On the pop-up menu, you'll get a menu item and a pop-out menu. You'll get the following options depending on the data type of the column:

Text Filters - this is available when the column has a text field or has a mixture of text and numbers: Equals, Does Not Equal, Begins With, Ends With, or Contains.

Number Filters - this option is only available when the column contains only numbers: Equals, Does Not Equal, Greater Than, Less Than, or Between.

Date Filters - this option is only available when the column contains only dates: Last Week, Next Month, This Month, and Last Month. *Clear Filter from 'Column name'* - this option is only available if a filter has already been applied to the column. Select this option to clear the filter.

When you select any of the first 3 options, you will get a dialog box – *Custom AutoFilter*. You'll be specifying your custom filter conditions using this screen.

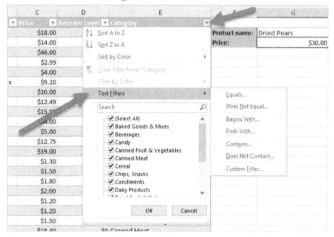

For example, if you wanted to display data with a price range between $2 and $10, you would:

Click on the *Price* AutoFilter and then select *Number Filters > Between…* from the pop-up menu.

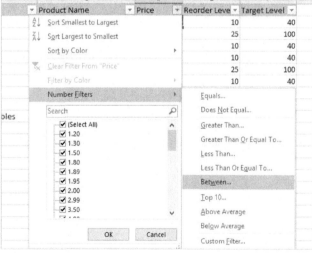

The *Custom AutoFilter* screen allows you to enter the criteria and specify the condition.

Enter the values you want to use for the filter. In our example, the values would be $2 and $10. Select the logical operator. In this case, we'll need *And*, as both conditions must be true. Price >= $2 *And* <= $10. If only one of either condition needs to be true, then you would select *Or*.

Click OK when done.

The data will now be filtered to only show records where the price is between $2 and $10.

Changing the Sort Order of a Filtered List

To change the sort order of the filtered results, click the *AutoFilter* icon that appears on the column used for the filter.

Select Sort Largest to Smallest or Sort Smallest to Largest. *For a text column, it would be* Sort A to Z *or* Sort Z to A.

Removing a Filter Select any cell in the range/table and click on *Clear* in the *Sort & Filter* group. The filter will be removed, and all data will be displayed.

Freeze Pane

When you have a large worksheet with lots of data, you may want your data headers (row and/or column) to remain visible as you scroll down or to the right of the page.

To make your column headings always visible, you can freeze them on the page so that the scroll action does not take them out of view.

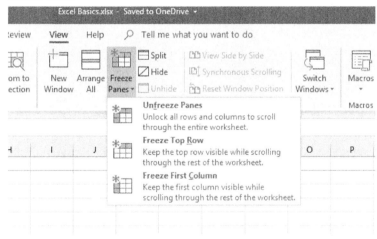

How to Freeze Columns and rows

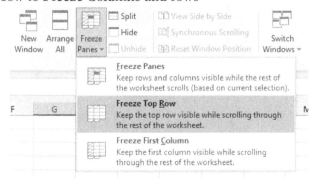

Now, you may want to freeze columns and rows in your Microsoft Excel highlight the cells below the rows. Go to the right of the columns you want to keep visible when you are scrolling.

Tap on the *View icon*. From the list, you can click on *Freeze panes*.

Splitting a Window into several Panes

Here are the methods of splitting a window into different panes:

1. Choose under the row where you want the split to occur.

2. Another method is clicking the column to the right of where you desire the split.

3. Go to the *View menu* in the *Window group* and select the *Split icon*.

4. If you want to take away the split panes, tap on the *Split Again menu*.

Freeze the top row of your worksheet:

In the Window group, click on *Freeze Panes* and select *Freeze Top Row*.

When you now scroll down the page, the top row will always remain visible.

Freeze the first column of your worksheet:

In the Window group, click on *Freeze Panes* and select *Freeze First Column*.

When you now scroll to the right of the page, the first column will always remain visible.

On some occasions, you may want to freeze rows and columns other than the first ones.

Freeze any row of your choosing:

Place the cell pointer directly under the row you want to freeze to make it the active cell.

Click on the *View* tab.

In the Window group, click on *Freeze Panes* and select *Freeze Panes* from the pop-up list.

Freeze any column of your choosing:

Select a cell on the first row of the column that's to the right of the one you want to freeze. If you want to freeze column C, for example, then you would select cell D1.

Click on the *View* tab.

In the Window group, click on *Freeze Panes* and select *Freeze Panes* from the pop-up list.

Unfreeze panes

To unfreeze any frozen row or columns, click on Freeze Panes and select *Unfreeze Panes* from the pop-up menu.

Other examples:

If you want to freeze only rows 1 and 2, you will select cell *A3* and select *View > Freeze Panes > Freeze Panes*.

If you want to freeze only columns A and B, you will click on cell *C1* and select *View > Freeze Panes > Freeze Panes*.

Create Drop-Down Menus

Start by adding content to a worksheet in contiguous cells.

Assign a name to the data as if you were creating a table.

Select the cell that you wish for the dropdown menu to be connected to.

Choose the Data tab followed by the Data Validation option found in the Data Tools grouping.

Under the Settings tab, look for the box named Source and enter the name of your list preceded by the = sign.

Under the Input Message tab, enter a title and any additional message you want the dropdown list to display.

Check the box offering In-Cell Dropdown and select OK.

You can also include a variety of error alerts to prevent incorrect data from being entered into the cell.

When you click on the cell in question, the new dropdown box should then appear.

Data Consolidation: Make The Same Change Across Multiple Worksheets

Data consolidation gives you the chance to combine multiple worksheets into a single one. You may combine data from separate worksheets in the same workbook, from distinct workbooks, or from both. The method enables you to pick the ranges from various sources that you wish to include in the consolidation, and Excel will aggregate the data in another worksheet. To consolidate data, all the ranges to be included in the consolidation have to be of the same shape and size. Assume we have sales data from 2017 to 2019 that we wish to combine from three worksheets into a single one titled "2017 – 2019 sales".

The three worksheets from which we will be combining data are as follows:

- 2017Sales.xlsx

- 2018Sales.xlsx

- 2019Sales.xlsx

To consolidate cell ranges from the three workbooks:

To begin, open the destination worksheet, which is the one into which you wish to combine your data. In our case, the file name will be "2017 – 2019 sales".

Now open the source workbooks. They are the 3 workbooks mentioned above containing the information to be consolidated. Change to the worksheet where you wish to merge your data. Click the *Data* tab, then the *Data Tools* group, and then the *Consolidate* button. The Consolidate dialog box will appear.

To close the dialog box, click the *Collapse Dialog* button (at the right side of the *Reference* field). When you click this button, it will minimize the Consolidate dialog box.

Choose now the range from the first worksheet.

Select the first workbook containing data you want to consolidate in the final workbook named "2017 – 2019 sales". The workbook will now be the active window.

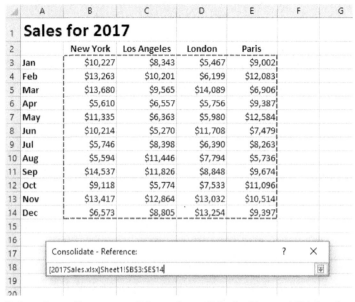

Select the cells to consolidate, then click the Expand Dialog button to enlarge the Consolidate dialog box.

Click *Add* to add the selected range to the *All references* list box.

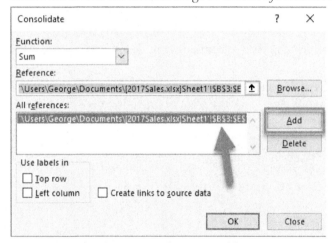

Repeat the previous procedures to add more ranges to the consolidation. These ranges can originate from various workbooks or different worksheets within the same workbook.

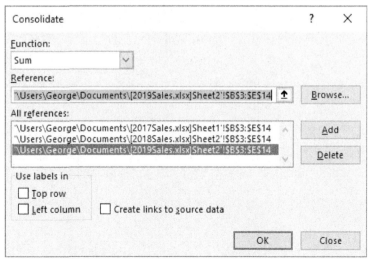

Note: *Sum* is the default function for aggregating data in the consolidated worksheet. By choosing the Function drop-down list and selecting a different function, you can convert this to another function, such as *Average or Count*.

When you've added all of the ranges to be consolidated, click OK.

	A	B	C	D	E
1	Sales for 2017 - 2019				
2		New York	Los Angeles	London	Paris
3	Jan	$29,515	$27,631	$29,693	$19,726
4	Feb	$33,126	$30,064	$18,811	$26,229
5	Mar	$38,592	$34,477	$41,211	$30,876
6	Apr	$18,162	$22,023	$18,734	$22,527
7	May	$31,523	$29,097	$20,000	$25,832
8	Jun	$35,671	$23,079	$24,754	$36,707
9	Jul	$28,859	$34,226	$26,289	$27,339
10	Aug	$18,148	$39,842	$29,510	$29,486
11	Sep	$26,687	$32,604	$24,378	$33,720
12	Oct	$38,590	$19,248	$26,325	$29,174
13	Nov	$23,903	$30,672	$35,400	$38,724
14	Dec	$20,449	$33,015	$24,878	$24,997

Each cell in the consolidated data will now hold the sum for that cell from all the other worksheets.

CHAPTER 5: PAGE SET UP AND PRINTING

How To Print An Excel Spreadsheet

Most importantly, we'll go over some undeniable-level Excel printing rules. From that point onward, we'll zero in on the most vital parts.

Assuming you wish to print an Excel accounting page, adhere to these guidelines:

To print your worksheet, go to File > Print or press Ctrl + P. As a result, you'll be brought to the Print Preview window.

In the Copies box, type the number of duplicates you'll require.

From the Printer drop-down choice, pick a printer to utilize.

Under Settings, you might modify the page borders, direction, paper size, and different choices to print definitively what you need.

Press the Print button to print.

Choose Whether To Print The Conclusion, A Single Sheet, Or The Entire Workbook.

To train Excel which data and components ought to be associated with the printout, click the bolt close to Print Active Sheets under Settings and pick one of the accompanying choices:

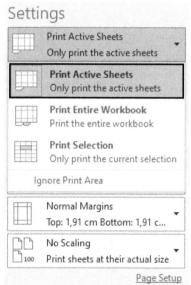

Below is a quick explanation of each parameter seen in the screen capture above, as well as how to utilize them correctly.

Print Selection / Range

To print a specific range of cells, select it on the sheet and then select Print Selection. Hold the Ctrl key down when selecting non-adjoining cells or reaches.

Print Entire Sheet(S)

To print the total sheet that is currently open, select Print Active Sheets.

Hold down the Ctrl key while tapping on the sheet tabs to print a couple of sheets, then, at that point, select Print Active Sheets.

Print Entire Workbook

Select Print Entire Workbook to print all sheets in the current Workbook.

Print Excel Table

To print an Excel table, chose Print Specified Row from the menu by right-clicking any cell in the table. This option only appears when a table or section is selected.

How To Print The Same Range In Multiple Sheets

When working with spreadsheets that aren't perfectly aligned, such as sales or marketing figures, you should print similar information throughout all of them. Here's the quickest way to go about it:

Open the main sheet and select the reach to print.

Click on extra sheet tabs to be printed while holding down the Ctrl key. Click the essential sheet tab, hold the Shift key, and snap the last sheet tab to choose adjoining sheets.

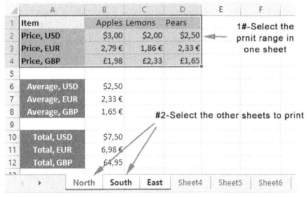

Click Ctrl + P and pick Print Selection in the drop-down list right under Settings.

Click the Print button.

Tip. Check the number of pages at the bottom of the Preview section to be sure Excel will print the information you want. Assuming that each sheet has just one territory, the number of pages should correspond to the number of sheets selected. If at least two territories are selected, each will be printed on a separate page, increasing the number of pages equal to the number of reaches. Use the right and passed-on bolts to travel through each printing page see for complete control.

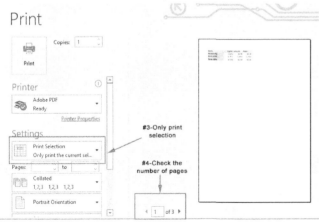

Tip. To set the print region in different sheets, you can utilize these Print Area macros.

How To Print Excel Spreadsheet On One Page

Excel, by default, prints sheets at their original size. Similarly, the larger the worksheet, the more pages it will require. Choose one of the following Scaling options at the end of the Settings segment in the Print Preview box to print an Excel sheet on one page:

Fit Sheet on One Page - this will contract the sheet so it fits on one page.

Fit All Columns on One Page - this will print all of the segments on a single page, however, the lines may be split across many pages.

Fit All Rows on One Page - this will print every one of the lines on one page, however, the sections might reach out to various pages.

To eliminate scaling, pick No Scaling in the rundown of choices.

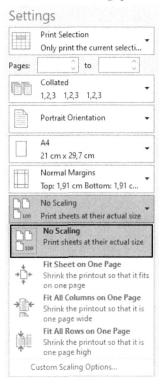

Please use extreme caution while printing on a single page; if you print on a large sheet, your output may become unreadable.

Click Custom Scaling Options... to see how much scaling will be used.

This will bring up the Page Setup dialog box, where you may double-check the number in the Adjust to box:

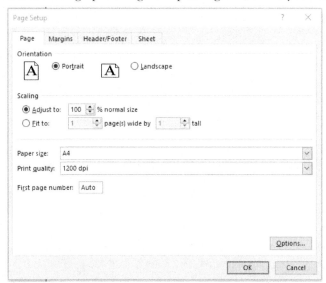

In the case that the Adjust To number is low, a printed copy will be difficult to read.

The following adjustments may be beneficial in this situation:

Change page direction. For spreadsheets with more lines than sections, the default Portrait orientation performs wonderfully. Change the page orientation to Landscape if your sheet has more sections than lines.

Change edges. The more modest the edges, the more space there will be for your information.

Determine the number of pages. On the Page tab of the Page Setup menu, under Scaling, enter the number of pages in both Fit to boxes to print an Excel accounting page on a specified number of pages (wide and tall). If it's not too much bother, keep in mind that using this option ignores any manual page breaks.

Print To File – Save The Output For Later Use

Print to File is one of the most neglected Excel print features, with a big proportion of individuals overlooking it. To put it another way, this option saves the result to a file rather than sending it to a printer.

What makes you think you'd need to print a document? When extra printed duplicates of a comparable record are necessary, this saves time. The idea is that you create the print settings (edges, direction, page breaks, and so on) only once and save the outcome as a.pdf file. Simply open that.pdf document and select Print the next time you need a printed copy.

We should examine how that functions:

On the Page Layout tab, arrange the necessary print settings and press Ctrl + P.

In the Print Preview window, open the Printer drop-down list, and select Print to File.

Click the Print button.

Pick where to save a .png document containing the result.

Print Preview In Excel

To avoid unexpected consequences, it's always a good idea to check yields before printing. There are a couple of ways to acquire a print review in Excel:

Click File > Print.

Press the print to see easy route Ctrl + P or Ctrl + F2.

When it comes to conserving paper, ink, and stress, Dominate Print Preview is a lifesaver. It not only shows how your worksheets will appear on paper, but it also allows you to make specific changes directly in the preview window:

Use the right and left bolts at the bottom of the window to examine the next and previous pages, or input the page number in the container and click Enter. When a sheet or reach has more than one printed page of information, the bolts may appear.

Click the Show Margins button in the bottom right corner to reveal the page boundaries. To make the margins larger or smaller, use the mouse to move them. You may also adjust the segment width by pulling the handles at the top or bottom of the print, as shown in the window.

Although Excel Print Preview does not include a zoom slider, you may zoom using the standard alternative method of Ctrl + scroll wheel. Click the Zoom to Page button in the lower-right corner to return to the original size.

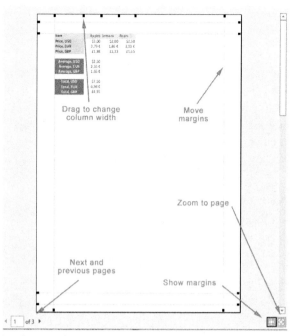

To leave Print Preview and return to your worksheet, click the bolt in the upper left corner of the Print Preview window.

Excel Print Options And Features

The Print Preview window, which we looked at before, contains the most often used print options. On the Page Layout tab of the Excel lace, there are a lot more options:

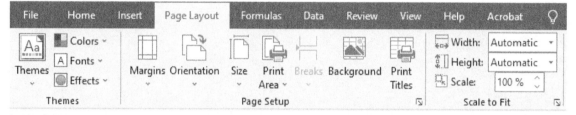

Aside from setting page margins and paper size, you can also embed and remove page breaks, select print region, hide and reveal gridlines, choose which lines and segments to repeat on each printed page, and that's only the beginning.

In the Page Setup exchange box, you may access advanced options for which there is no room on the strip. Click the conversation launcher in the Page Setup group on the Page Layout tab to access it.

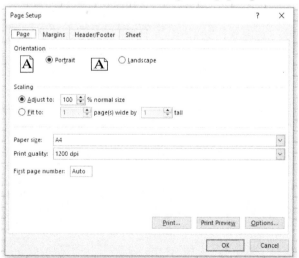

Note that the Page Setup option can also be accessed through the Print Preview window. A section of the options, such as Print region or Rows to rehash at the top, maybe disabled in this case. Open the Page Setup exchange from the Page Layout tab to enable these features.

Excel Print Area

Set the print section to ensure that just a portion of your accounting page is printed, rather than the entire page. How it's done is as follows:

Select at least one territories that you need to print.

On the Page Layout tab, in the Page Setup bunch, click Print Area > Set Print Area.

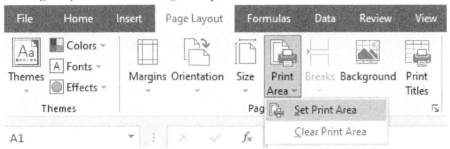

When you save the workout manual, the Print Area setting is preserved. As a result, whenever you print this particular sheet, a printed copy will only include the print region.

If it's not too much bother, look for further information. In Excel, how to set the print region.

How To Add A Print Button To Excel Quick Access Toolbar

If you frequently print in Excel, having the Print order on the Quick Access Toolbar might be quite useful. Simply follow the steps below to accomplish this:

Click the Customize Quick Access Toolbar button (the down bolt at the furthest right of the Quick Access toolbar).

In the rundown of the shown orders, select Print Preview and Print. Done!

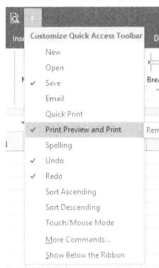

How To Insert Page Breaks In Excel

By integrating page breaks within a large bookkeeping page, you may choose how the information is split across many pages. The following is a well-guarded secret:

Click on the line or section that you need to move to another page.

On the Page Layout tab, in the Page Setup bunch, click Breaks > Insert Page Break.

A page break is embedded.

To outwardly see what information falls on various pages, change to the View tab and empower Page Break Preview.

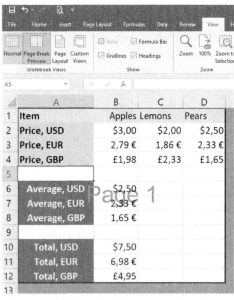

If you need to reposition a page break, just drag the brake line to the desired location.

For further information, see How to embed and remove page breaks in Excel.

How To Print Formulas In Excel

To enable Excel to publish formulas rather than their calculated results, just present the equation in a spreadsheet and then print it to no one's surprise.

Change to the Formulas page and click the Show Formulas button in the Formula Auditing group to complete the task.

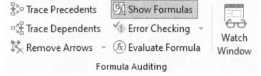

How To Print A Chart In Excel

Select the diagram of interest and press Ctrl + P to print simply the graph without the worksheet information. On the right side of the Print Preview box, you'll notice a graph review and the Print Selected Chart option selected under Settings. If the view appears to be what you want, click Print; if not, modify the settings to:

Tips and notes:

To print all of a sheet's contents, including the diagram, press Ctrl + P without selecting anything on the page, and make sure the Print Active Sheets option is selected under Settings.

It's unrealistic to change the scaling of an outline in the Print Preview window. On the off chance that you wish the printed outline to fit the full page, resize your diagram to make it greater.

How To Print Gridlines In Excel

Of course, all worksheets are printed without gridlines. To print an Excel bookkeeping page with lines between your cells, this is what you want to do:

Change to the Page Layout tab.

in the Sheet Options bunch, under Gridlines, check the Print box.

What to change the printed gridlines shading? The nitty-gritty guidelines can be found in How to make Excel print gridlines.

How To Print Titles In Excel

Finding out what either information means in a multi-page Excel file may be intriguing. The Print Titles feature allows you to display the section and column headings on each printed page, making it much easier to read a printed copy.

To rehash the header line or header segment on each printed page, do these means:

On the Page Layout tab, in the Page Setup bunch, click Print Titles.

On the Sheet tab of the Page Setup discourse box, under Print titles, indicate which lines to rehash at the top as well as which segments to rehash at left.

When done, click OK.

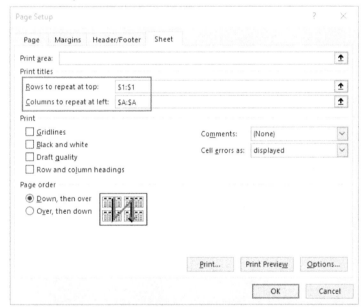

For more data, if it's not too much trouble, perceive How to print lines and segment headers on each page.

How To Print Comments In Excel

If your notes are as important as the facts on the accounting page, you may want to write them down as well. Do the following as a result of this:

On the Page Layout tab, in the Page Setup bunch, click the discourse launcher (a little bolt in the lower-right corner of a gathering).

In the Page Setup window, change to the Sheet tab, click the bolt close to Comments, and pick how you need them printed:

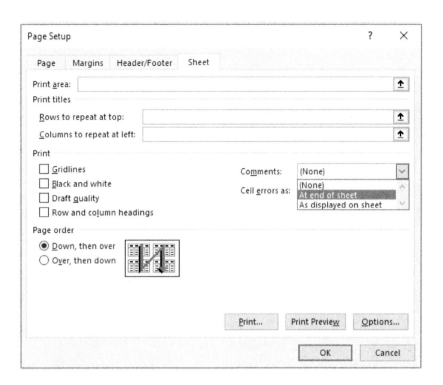

For additional subtleties, kindly perceive How to print remarks in Excel.

How To Print Address Labels From Excel

Use the Mail Merge feature in Excel to produce mailing labels. If it's not too much work, plan ahead of time that getting the names correct on the first try may take some time. In this educational activity, you can observe the basic necessary procedures with a lot of helpful hints: Excel may be used to create and print names.

MODULE C

CHAPTER 6: EXCEL TABLES

How To Create Tables

This is the first step in learning how to work with Excel tables and their features and tools. Create a list with column headings and row headings if they are needed by clicking on Insert then table on the program. You need to visually confirm that you have the right number of columns and rows. If it is ok, click on the *My Table Has Headers* checkbox, and then ok. This will give you a formatted Excel table. If there is a particular table format that you want to create, instead of going to insert, go to Home, then choose a table style from the gallery provided.

Select a cell from the data list you prepared.

Click the Insert tab from the *Ribbon*.

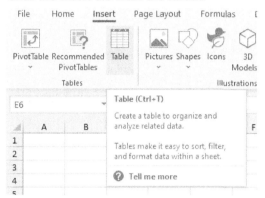

Select the *Table* command from the *Tables* group.

The range for your data should appear automatically in the Create Table dialogue box, and the *My table has a headers* option that should be checked. You can change the range and check the box if necessary.

To accept these settings, click OK.

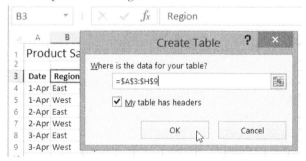

How To Apply Formatting To The Table

Select a cell within the table.

On the *Table Design* tab, locate the *Table Styles* group and click on the drop-down button for the styles. A drop-down menu will show you more styles.

Mouse over each style to see a preview of how it would look on your worksheet.

Table Style Options

Here you have several options for configuring the style of your table.

For example, you can change your table from *Banded Row* to *Banded Columns*. Banded rows are the alternating colors applied to your table rows.

Banded Rows are the default, but if you want banded columns instead, uncheck *Banded Rows* and check *Banded Columns* to have your columns alternate in color instead of your rows.

Note that if a new column or row is added to the table, it will inherit the current table style automatically. When you add a new row, any formulas applied to your table will also be copied to the new row.

Enter Data Into An Existing Excel Table

You don't have to keep the table
Excel tables are usually very neat; that is why a lot of people prefer to format their data in tables. It also saves them so much time, and the features that one can access in a table are more than they can get elsewhere. That is why it is very useful. However, if you do not want your data to be in a table afterward, you can always ditch the table, keeping the neat format. To do this, click inside the table after you have formatted your data, go to table tools, convert to the range, and then ok.

Adding new rows to the table
Click on the cell that is at the bottom on the right side of the table, then press Tab. It is very simple, and you can do this several times if you need more rows on your table.

If you want to add more rows or columns to the end of the table, drag the small indicator that appears at the bottom right corner of the table.

If you want an additional row inside a table, click just where the row should appear, then click home, the insert, and then insert table row above/below or home. With this, the table will be formatted automatically in order to accommodate the new row.

How You Can Sort And Filter Data

Sorting Data in a Table

Before you begin sorting data, ensure there are no blank rows and blank columns.

Tip: To spot blank rows or columns, select a cell within the data and press *CTRL + A*. Then press for a few times "." + *CTRL*. This moves the cursor around the four corners of the range so you can see the whole area.

Sort by One Column To quickly sort by one column in your table:

Carry out the following steps to apply a custom sort:

Select any cell within the data.

On the *Ribbon*, navigate to *Home > Sort & Filter* (in the Editing group).

Select *Custom Sort...* from the drop-down menu. The sort dialog box will be displayed.

Tip: Another way to launch the Custom Sort screen is to click on *Data > Sort* (in the Sort & Filter group).

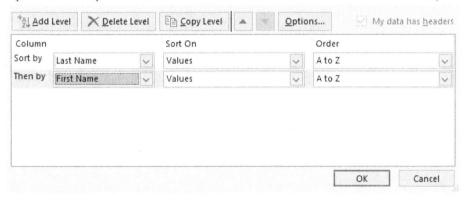

Click on Add Level.

Under *Column*, select the column you want to sort from the drop-down list. Select the second column you want to include in the sort in the *Then by* field. For example, *Sort by Last Name* and *First Name*.

Under *Sort On*, select *Values*.

Under *Order*, select the order you want to sort on, i.e., *A to Z* for ascending order and *Z to A* for descending order.

Click *OK* when done.

Filtering Table Data

Excel provides an array of options to filter your data so that you can view data that meets a certain criterion. Filters provide a quick way to work with a subset of data in a range or table. When you apply the filter, you temporarily hide some of the data so that you can focus on the data you need to view.

How to filter data:

Click on *Home > Sort & Filter > Filter* (or click *Data > Filter*).

You will get filter arrows at the top of each column.

Open the drop-down menu by clicking the arrow of the column you want to filter. For example, Price.

Uncheck *Select All* and check the values you want to use for the filter.

Click *OK*.

The filter drop-down arrow changes to a funnel icon to show that the column is filtered. If you look at the row heading numbers, you'll see that they're now blue, indicating which rows are included in the filtered data. To remove the filter, click on *Clear* in the *Sort & Filter* group. The filter will be removed, and all data will be displayed.

Applying a Custom Filter Select the filter drop-down arrow and then select one from the following:

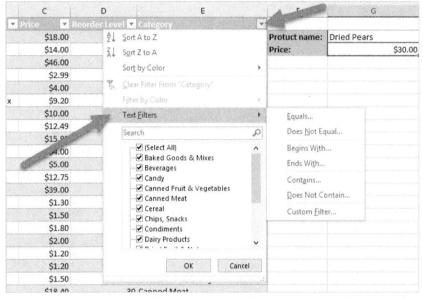

Text Filters - this is available when the column has a text field or has a mixture of text and numbers: Equals, Does Not Equal, Begins With, Ends With, or Contains.

Number Filters - this option is only available when the column contains only numbers: Equals, Does Not Equal, Greater Than, Less Than, or Between.

Date Filters - this option is only available when the column contains only dates: Last Week, Next Month, This Month, and Last Month.

Clear Filter from 'Column name' - this option is only available if a filter has already been applied to the column. Select this option to clear the filter.

When you select any of the first 3 options, you will get a dialog box – Custom AutoFilter.

Choose *And* if both conditions have been considered to filter. Alternatively, select Or if only one of the conditions needs to be true.

Enter the values you want to use for the filter.

For example, to view rows with a number that is within a certain range, select *Number Filters > Between* and then enter the values in the two boxes provided.

For the example in the image above, we're filtering the **Price** column so that only rows between $2 and $10 are shown.

To change the order of the filtered results, click the filter drop-down button and then select *Sort Largest to Smallest* or *Sort Smallest to Largest*.

For a text sort column, it would be *Sort A to Z* or *Sort Z to A*.

Filtering Table with Slicer

Slicers are visual filters for tables, pivot tables, and pivot charts in Excel. Slicers work well with dashboards and summary reports because of their visual properties, but they can be used everywhere to make data sifting quicker and simpler.

Here below the steps to create a Slicer for your table:

Click on your table.

Then click Insert Slicer in the Tools (Table Design tab)

Mark the checkboxes for the columns you wish to filter in the Insert Slicers dialog box.

Click OK.

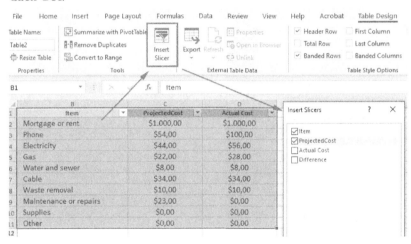

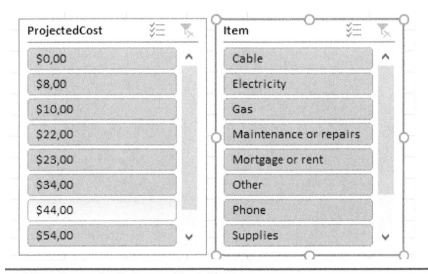

Adding Rows Or Columns To A Table

To add totals to your table:

Select a cell in a table. Select *Table Design > Total Row.*

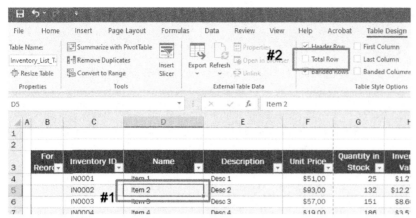

On the total row drop-down list, you have a choice of functions to select from, like *Average, Count Numbers, Max, Sum, Var,* and more.

Tip: If you need to add a new row of data to your table at some later point, you need to uncheck *Total Row* on the *Table Design* tab, add the new row, and then recheck *Total Row.*

CHAPTER 7: CHARTS

Choose A Chart Type

Click the *Insert* button. Recommended Charts are focused on prominence, but you can choose a different template by clicking either of the dropdown menus.

Types Of Chart

Column Charts

Column charts, for example, are ideal for comparing data or where you have several categories with a single variable (for instance, a variety of products or genres). Clustered, 3-D clustered, stacked, 3-D stacked, 100 percent stacked, 3-D 100 % stacked, and 3-D are the seven-column chart forms available in Excel. Choose the visualization that best tells the story of your results.

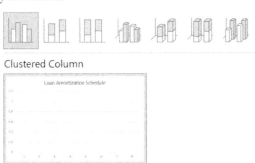

Clustered Column

Bar Charts

The major difference between a bar chart and a column chart is that the bars in a bar chart are horizontal rather than vertical. While bar charts and column charts may also be used interchangeably, some people choose column charts when dealing with negative values because it's simpler to represent negatives vertically on a y-axis.

Clustered Bar

Pie Charts

To contrast percentages of a whole (the sum of the values of your data), use pie charts. Each value is expressed by a pie slice, allowing you to see the proportions. There are five varieties of pie charts: pie, pie of pie (which divides one pie into two to indicate sub-category proportions), 3-D pie, bar of pie & doughnut.

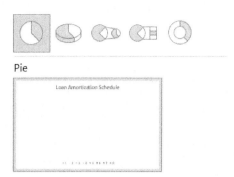

Pie

Line Charts

Instead of static data points, a line chart is best for displaying trends over time. The lines connect each data point, allowing you to see if the value(s) improved or decreased over time. The seven-line chart choices are line, stacked line, 100 percent stacked line, stacked line with markers, line with markers, 100 percent stacked line with markers, and 3-D line.

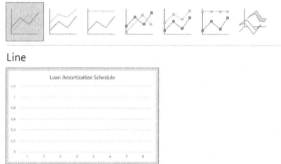

Line

Scatter Charts

Scatter charts are used to display how one variable influences another. They are similar to line graphs in that they are helpful for displaying improvement in variables over time. (This is referred to as correlation.) Bubble charts, which are a common chart category, are classified as scatter. Seven choices: the first one scatter, the second one scatter with smooth lines, the third one scatter with smooth lines and markers, the fourth one scatter with straight lines and markers, the fifth one scatter with straight lines, the sixth one bubble, & last one 3-D bubble.

Scatter

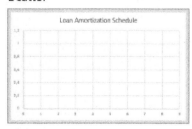

Make Your Chart

Let's select the data we want to create a chart for.

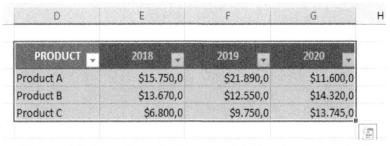

Select Clustered Column from the *Recommended Charts* button on the *Insert* tab.

Excel can generate a clustered chart column based on the data you've chosen. The map will appear in the workbook's center.

To give your chart a name, double-click the Chart Title text and enter a title.

This graph would be referred to as *"Products Profit 2018 to 2020"*.

The rest of the walkthrough will be based on this chart.

PRODUCT	2018	2019	2020
Product A	$15.750,0	$21.890,0	$11.600,0
Product B	$13.670,0	$12.550,0	$14.320,0
Product C	$6.800,0	$9.750,0	$13.745,0

Chart Design and Format are the two sections on the toolbar that you can use to make changes to your chart.

Excel applies to style, layout; format presets to charts & graphs by default; however, you can customize them by going through the tabs.

Following that, we'll take you through all of the Chart Design options.

Add Chart Elements

By adding chart elements to the graph or chart, you may improve it. By using the *Add Chart* Feature dropdown menu in the upper left corner, you can choose a chart element (beneath the *Home* tab).

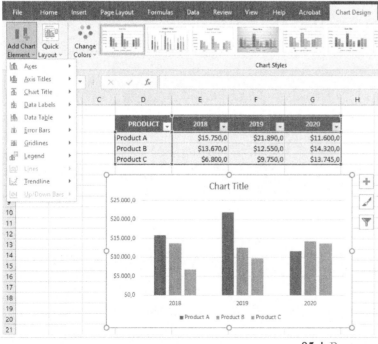

Axes: Display Or Hide

Axes can be chosen. To view both horizontally and vertically axes on your chart, Excel will automatically pull the row and column headers from your chosen cell set (Primary Horizontal & Primary Vertical have a checkmark next to them under Axes.)

To remove the view axis from your chart, uncheck these choices. In this case, selecting *Primary Vertical* will delete the year labels from your chart's horizontal axis.

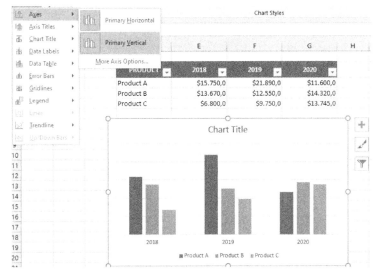

More Axis Options... opens a window with additional text and formatting options, such as labels or numbers, or changing text color and height, inserting tick marks, from the Axes dropdown selection.

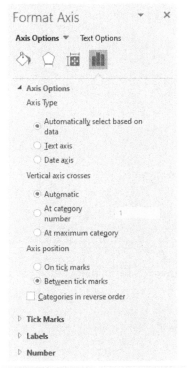

Add Axis Titles

Select Axis Titles from the dropdown menu after clicking Add Chart Element. Since axis names are not immediately added to charts in Excel, both Primary Horizontal & Primary Vertical would be unchecked.

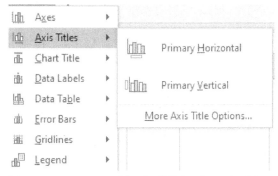

In this case, we pressed both. Fill in the axis titles. The titles Year (horizontal) and Profit (vertical) were inserted in this example.

To Remove Or Relocate A Chart Title

Select Chart Title from the Add Chart Element dropdown menu. *None, Above Chart, Oriented Overlay,* and *More Title Options* are the four options available. To remove the chart title, choose *None.* To put the title above the chart, click *Above Chart.* Excel can automatically put a chart title above the chart if you make one.

To put the title inside the chart's gridlines, choose *Centered Overlay.* This option can be used with caution: you do not want the title to obscure any of your data or complicate your graph (as in the example below).

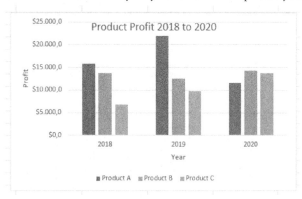

Add Data Labels

Select *Data Table* from the *Add Chart Element* dropdown menu. From here, you can use three pre-formatted choices as well as an extended menu.

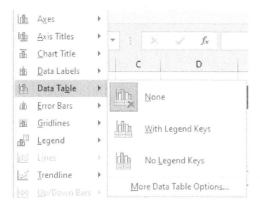

The default setting is None, which means that the data table is not duplicated inside the chart.

Add Error Bars

Select *Error Bars* from the *Add Chart Element* menu. There are four choices in addition to More Error Bars Options: None, Standard Error, 5% (Percentage), & Standard Deviation. Using various standard equations for isolating error, error bars offer a visual representation of the possible error in the displayed results.

When we choose Standard Error from the choices, we get a chart similar to the one shown below.

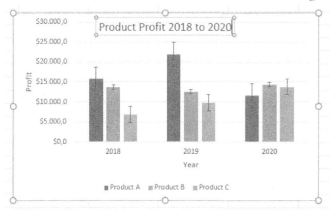

Add Gridlines

Gridlines may be added to a chart by clicking Add Chart Element and then Gridlines. There are four variations: *Primary Major Vertical, Primary Major Horizontal, Primary Minor Vertical,* and *Primary Minor Horizontal,* in addition to *More Grid Line Options.* Excel automatically adds *Primary Major Horizontal* gridlines to a column table.

Here's what our map looks like when all four gridline choices are selected.

Add Legend

Select *Legend* from the *Add Chart Element* dropdown menu. There are five legend positioning options in addition to *More Legend Preferences: None, Top, Right, Left, and Bottom.*

The type and format of your chart will determine where the legend is placed. Select the alternative that appears to be the most appealing on your graph. Selecting the *Right legend* placement, this is what our chart looks like.

Add Lines

Clustered column charts do not support lines. However, in some chart categories where you are just comparing two variables, you should add lines to the chart by checking the right choice (like target, reference, average, etc.).

Add A Trendline

Select Trendline from the Add Chart Element dropdown menu. There are five choices: None, Linear, Linear Forecast, Exponential, and Moving Average, in addition to More Trendline Options.

Excel provides a trendline for each commodity when we're evaluating 3 separate products over time. Let's select the *Linear* trendline, click 2018, and then the OK button.

Below is what we will obtain: a dotted trendline will now appear on the chart to reflect Product A's linear progression. Linear (Product A) has now been applied to the legend in Excel.

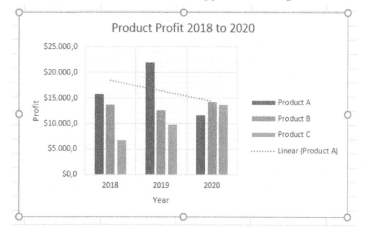

Double-click the Trendline to see the trendline equation on your table. On the right side of your PC, a Format Trendline window may appear. The equation is now visible on your graph.

Note: You can make as many trendlines as you like with each attribute in your table. Just repeat the previous process. Here's an example of a chart of trendlines for 2018 and 2019.

Add Up Or Down Bars

Up/Down Bars are not accessible in a column chart, but they may be used to display increases & decreases among data points in a line chart.

Adjust The Quick Layout

The fast layout is the second dropdown menu on the toolbar, and it helps you to easily adjust the layout of your chart's components (titles, legend, clusters, etc.).

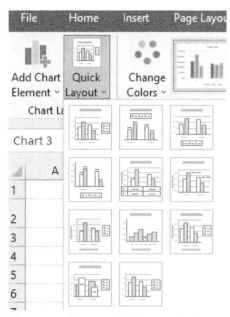

There are eleven quick layout choices to choose from. Hover your cursor over the various choices for a description, then choose the one you want to use.

Alter The Colors

Click the *Change Colors* button in the *Chart Style* tab. You can choose a wide range of colors combination for your bars.

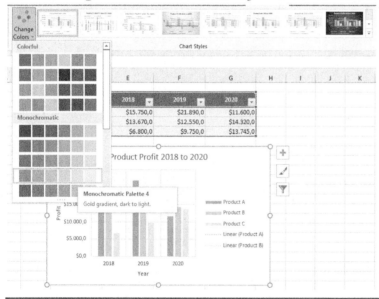

Alter The Style

There are 14 chart forms used for cluster column charts. The chart will be shown in Style 1 by design; however, you may adjust it to either of the other types. To see further choices, click the arrow to the right of the picture bar.

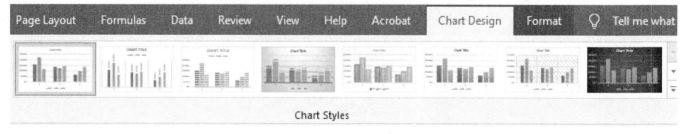

Change The Row/Column Order

To rotate the axes, press the Switch Row/Column button on the toolbar. Notice those flipping axes for each chart. For instance, if you have more than two variables, it is not always intuitive.

Switch Row/
Column

Switching the row and column, in this case, flips the product & year (profit remains on the y-axis). The graph is now organized by product (rather than by year), and the color-coded legend corresponds to the year (not product). To avoid some doubt, go to the legend and shift the Series to Year's names.

Select The Data

To adjust the context of your files, click the Select Data icon on the toolbar.

Select
Data

A window can swing wide. Click the OK button after you've typed in the cell set you like. The graph will refresh automatically to display the latest data set.

Modify The Chart Type

Change the chart type from the dropdown menu.

You may adjust the chart category to each of Excel's nine chart types from here. Of necessity, double-check that the data is suitable for the chart format you've chosen.

By pressing Save as Template, you can save your chart as a template.

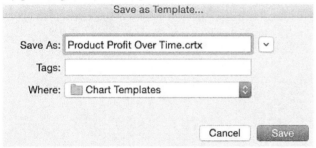

Move The Chart

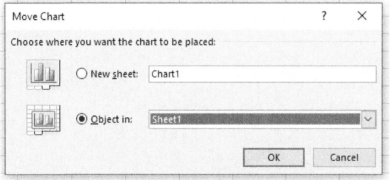

Modify The Formatting

You may adjust the colors, scale, design, fill, and orientation of all elements and text in the table and insert shapes using the Format tab. To make a chart that represents your company's brand, go to the Format tab and then use the shortcuts accessible (colors, images, etc.).

Select the chart feature you want to update from the dropdown menu on the top-left corner of the toolbar.

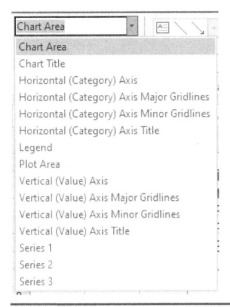

Delete Chart

Simply choose a chart and press the Delete key on the keyboard to delete it.

Printing Charts

To print a chart on a separate chart sheet in a workbook file, enable the chart sheet by clicking the sheet tab, then press *CTRL+P* to open the *Print* panel, where Print Active Sheet(s) appears as the default selection for the Settings drop-down option box.

- *Draft Quality:* Clik this to print the map using the draft-quality setting on your printer.

- *Print in Black and White:* Check this box to get the map printed in black and white on your color printer.

CHAPTER 8: SHAPES, SMARTART AND IMAGES

Shapes

To draw anything from shapes in Excel, choose any of the shapes you want to create, hold left-click drag, create your shape in the desired size, and then release the key to get the finished drawing.

How to Change a Shape

Left-click on the shape that you want to change. Press and hold CTRL to select more than one shape at the same time.

Go to the *Shape Format* tab, and click *Edit Shape* in the *Insert Shapes* group.

Select *Change Shape*, and then click the shape that you want.

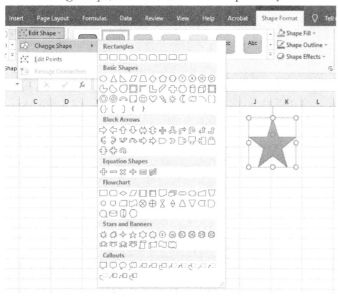

Smart Art

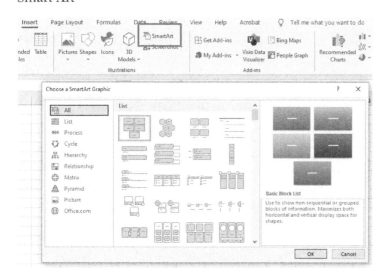

Smart Art Graphics are pre-made graphics in a spreadsheet or workbook displaying links, cycles, graphs, pyramids, and lists. These graphics do not contain or use pre-entered data from spreadsheets. Go to the Insert tab and select the Smart Art feature to add a Smart Art Graphic to your text (and type). The tab will appear in a highlighted green on your top toolbar, along with all of the graphic options, when you open it.

By pressing the button, you'll be able to use a graphic, which will appear on the spreadsheet you're working on. A small dialogue box will appear when you click on the image, giving you the option to change the data that will appear inside it. If you don't enter this dialogue box, the default text will appear in the graphic. If you accidentally close the dialogue box, select the button on the left-hand side of a graphic to open it back up on the screen.

Adding a smart art
Choose a design that you like.

The Smart art tool allows you to find the definition and further research of any word in any cell of a workbook. With this command, you can still search for images right inside the Excel workbook. If you want to use Smart art, click the cell containing a word followed by the Review tab. The next you are to do is click the Smart art command. You will see information about the word displayed by the right margin of your workbook. There are Define and Explore headings available. If you select Explore, it will give you research on the word, including images. The source of information is quoted.

Images

In your Excel spreadsheet, click where you want to put a picture.

Switch to the Insert tab > Illustrations group and click Pictures.

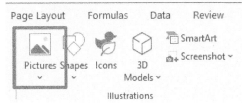

In the Insert Picture dialog that opens, browse to the picture of interest, select it, and click Insert.

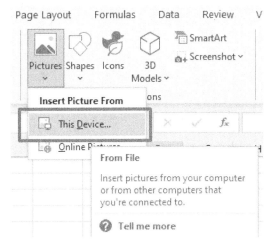

Add artistic effects to images

Like the most popular photo editing software programs, you can easily add effects to your images with Excel.

Double-click your image to open the Format tab, then choose the Artistic Effects option.

Select the creative effect you wish to use in your photograph.

CHAPTER 9: EXCEL TEMPLATES

In general, a prototype is a pattern that acts as a basis for another. An Excel blueprint is usually a specific type of file used as a premade or preformatted document for working with other worksheets. Excel provides you with some of the premade templates, or a user can make their own; doing so will require you to invest some time, but it will surely save you a lot of time later on.

<u>Exploring Excel template</u>: The easiest way to familiarize you with the Excel sample files is to hop in and check out others. Excel 2021 offers timely access to hundreds of prototype files.

<u>Viewing templates</u>: To explore the templates, click on *File* and then *New*

The prototype thumbnails that show on the screen are only a small selection of the ones available. Select one of your search words listed, or type in a specific term and check for more.

Enter the invoice, for instance, and press the Search button. Several thumbnails are shown in Excel. You may use the group filters on the right to narrow down the results. Given below is a sample invoice template.

How To Use Them

To build a template-based workbook, find a prototype that seems like it could be doing the job and tap on the thumbnail. Excel shows a box that includes a bigger version, the template source, and some extra material. If it still looks nice, press the key *Build*. If not, tap on one of your arrows to see information for the next (or previous) design in the list.

Clicking the *Create* button will allow Excel to import the prototype and then build a new workbook focused on that design. The operation you perform may vary according to the template. That prototype is specific, but much of it is self-explanatory. Many workbooks include tailoring. Substitute the details default with your own.

The following Figure shows a workbook built from a blueprint. In some ways, this workbook requires to be personalized. Once the template is used again, customizing it is more effective than any workbook generated from the template.

The one below is a workbook created from a template.

Use the save command for later use of this document. Excel provides a filename based on the prototype title, so you can choose whatever filename you choose.

Using Default Templates: Excel provides three types of using the file: the original template for the workbook. This type is being used as the base for new workbooks. The default template is used as a base for later use while working with other files.

These premade files of templates include formals that can be used while working with other files. It will help you to save time and work effortlessly.

MODULE D

CHAPTER 10: FORMULAS AND FUNCTIONS

When it comes to spreadsheets, the words function and formula are typically used interchangeably.

What Is A Formula?

A formula is an equation or expression that is designed to carry out calculations on values in the range of cells or a cell. A formula has to be written in a specific way, called **syntax**. The first element of the formula is always an equal sign (=), followed by the order of operations (parenthesis, exponents, multiplication, division, addition, and subtraction). As an example, the formula =A1+A2 adds the values of cells A1 and A2.

	A	B
1	1	=A1+A2
2	3	
3		

In the upper example, we entered the formula into cell B1, so the result, 4, will be shown there.

	A	B
1	1	4
2	3	

What Is A Function?

A function can be seen as a predefined formula. Just like the formula, the functions start with an equal sign (=) followed by the **function's name** and its **arguments**. The function name tells Excel what calculation is to be performed.

Functions help to remove the stress of having to manually enter a formula.

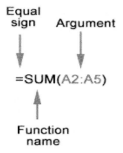

Equal sign / Argument

=SUM(A2:A5)

Function name

Example: The function =SUM (A2:A5) adds up all the values from A2 to A5.

	A	B	C	D	E
1	34				
2	56		=SUM(A2:A5)		
3	11		SUM(number1; [number2]; ...)		
4	72				
5	34				
6					

The result shown will be 173.

We will see in the following pages all the most important formulas and their use.

Elements Of Formulas

When creating a formula in Excel, you can utilize several components to give the source data to the formula and specify which operations should be done on that data. Depending on the sort of formula you generate, it could have any or all of the following components:

- **Constants**: values or numbers that you directly type, like $=5*2$

- **Cell references**: a link to a cell that contains the value you wish to use in a formula, e.g. $=SUM(A1+A2+A3+A4+A5)$. In order to refer to data contained in two or more adjacent cells, use a range reference like A1:A5. So to sum the values from cell A1 to cell A5, you can use the formula $=SUM(A1:A5)$

- **Names**: defined name for a cell range, constant, table, or function, for example $=SUM(your\_name)$

- **Functions**: Excel formulae that execute calculations based on the values specified in their arguments. We will deeply analyze them in the following pages.

- **Operators**: special symbols indicating the sort of operation or calculation to be done.

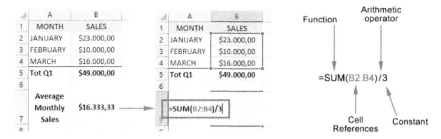

How To Enter A Formula

Let's go through an easy practical example to familiarize yourself with this. We want to sum up 3 values contained in the cells B1, B2, and B3.

Click the cell that you want the result to be shown; B4 in or example.

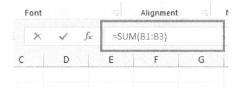

Go to the formula bar, click on it, and type your formula, starting with the equal sign (=). Remember that this specifies that your entry is a formula and not a static value.

In this case, the formula is $=SUM(B1:B3)$

Font			Alignment		
×	✓	*fx*	=SUM(B1:B3)		
C	D	E	F	G	

Press the Enter key, and you will get the result as shown below.

B4			×	✓	*fx*	=SUM(B1:B3)

	A	B	C	D	E	F
1		5				
2		20				
3		30				
4	TOT	55				

Tip: As much as possible, avoid typing cell references directly into the formula bar as it could introduce errors. So type in the equal sign followed by the function, and then an open bracket =SUM(. Then using your mouse pointer, select the cells you want for the arguments in the worksheet itself before typing in the closing bracket.

How To Enter A Function

You enter a function in the same way you enter a formula. All functions have an opening and closing bracket, and most functions have arguments enclosed in the brackets.

A *function argument* is a piece of data that a function needs in order to run. Most functions need at least one argument, but a select few, like the **Today()** and **Now()** functions, do not have arguments. To insert a function: Go to the cell where you need the result to appear and click on it. Click in the formula bar. *Start* entering an equal sign (=) and then type the function name. At this point, you'll get a dropdown list with all the Excel functions related to your entry.

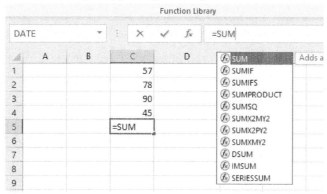

Use your up/down arrow keys to highlight the function you want on the list and, to select it, press the Tab key. This will enter the function and the opening bracket in the formula bar, enabling you to enter the argument(s).

Enter the argument(s) and the closing bracket, for example, =SUM(C1:C4).

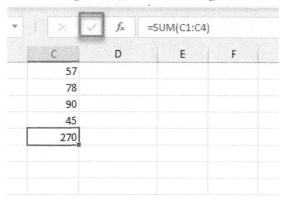

Click on *Enter* or press the *Enter* key to confirm your entry.

Tip: As much as possible, avoid typing cell references directly into the formula bar as it could introduce errors. Instead, enter the name of the formula and the open bracket; for example, enter *=SUM(*. Then select the cells you want for your argument in the worksheet itself before entering the closing bracket.

Using the Insert Function Dialog box

A second way you can enter a function is by using the *Insert Function* dialog box.

Click the *Insert Function* command on the *Formulas* tab or the *Insert Function* button next to the formula bar.

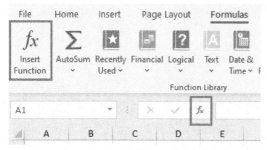

By doing this, the *Insert Function* dialog box will appear. This dialog box provides the option to search for the function or select it from a category.

To search for the function, enter the name of the function in the *Search for a function* box. As an example, if you were searching for the IF function, you would enter IF in the search box and click *Go*. The *Select a function* list will display all the functions related to your search term.

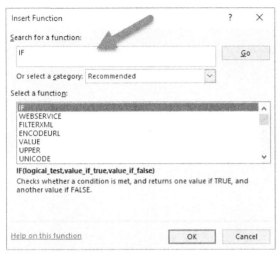

You can also use the *category* dropdown list to select a function if you know its category in Excel. For example, you can find the IF function in the *Logical* category.

If you have used a function recently, it'll be listed in the *Most Recently Used* category.

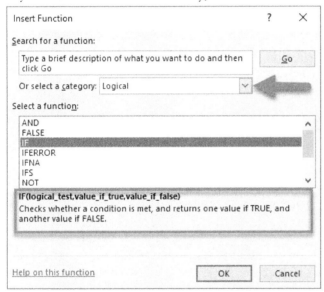

When you select a function on the list, you'll see the syntax for the function and a description of what the function does below the list.

Once you've selected the one you want, click *OK* to go to the *Functions Arguments* window.

The Functions Arguments window enables you to enter the arguments for the function. This dialog box is particularly useful if you are not familiar with a function because it provides a description of each argument, a preview of your entries, and the result returned by the function.

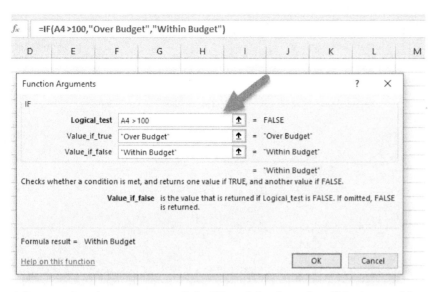

After entering the arguments, click *OK*, and the formula will be inserted into the formula bar.

Operators In Excel Formulas

Operators are special symbols to tell Excel what type of operation you want to perform in a formula. There are 4 types of operators: Arithmetic, Comparison (logical, Concatenation, Reference

Using Arithmetic operators in Excel formulas

These operators are used to execute elementary mathematical operations like addition, subtraction, multiplication, and division.

Operator	Meaning	Formula example
- (minus sign)	Subtraction Negation (reversing the sign)	=A2-B2 =-A2 (changes the sign of the value in A2)
+ (plus sign)	Addition	=A2+B2
/ (forward slash)	Division	=A2/B2
* (asterisk)	Multiplication	=A2*B2
% (percent sign)	Percentage	=A2*10% (returns 10% of the value in A2)
^ (caret)	Exponential (power of)	=A2^3 (raises the number in A2 to the power of 3)

Example: Let's say that you have to add the shipping cost (B2) to the production cost (A1) of a product.

=A2+B2

Using Comparison Operators in Excel formulas

Logical operators or *comparison operators* are used to comparing two values. The comparison always gives a logical result of TRUE or FALSE. Se below these operators

Comparison operator	Meaning	Formula example
=	Equal to	=A2=B2
<>	Not equal to	=A2<>B2
<	Less than	=A2<B2
>	Greater than	=A2>B2
<=	Less than or equal to	=A2<=B2
>=	Greater than or equal to	=A2>=B2

Example: The formula =C1=D1 will give you TRUE only if cells C1 and D1 contain the same value, which can be a number, a date, or a text. If not, the formula will return FALSE

Using the Text Concatenation operator in Excel formulas

The text concatenation operator is represented by the ampersand symbol (&). It can be used to combine two or more text strings into a single string. *Example:* If you have column A with names and column B with surnames, using the following formula, you can combine the first name and surname, and so on:

=A2&" "&B2

I used a space " " in between the two cell references to have a better result; otherwise, name and surname would be attacked.

Using Reference operators in Excel formulas

These operators are used to separate arguments in the formulas.

Colon (:)

It is a range operator that lets you create a single reference for multiple cells that are positioned between two cells you specify.

For example, the range B1:B50 has 50 cells included between the cells B1 and B50.

You may simply refer to the complete column (B:B) or row (2:2). For example, the formula =SUM(B:B) returns the sum of all the values in column B.

Comma (,)

It is used to separate arguments in the formulas.

Example: The formula =IF(A1>0, TRUE, FALSE) means that if A1 is greater than zero, return TRUE, otherwise FALSE.

Important note: In North America and certain other nations, the comma **(,)** is the default list separator. The comma is reserved as the decimal symbol in European nations, while the List Separator is commonly set to a semicolon **(;)**. In this case, semicolons have to be used to separate the parameters of a function. The above example, using the semicolons, would result =IF(A1>0; "True"; "False").

Since my readers may come from different countries, I thought it was nice and fun to use a comma sometimes and a semicolon at others (I have various licenses). Just remember to use what works for you!

Space

It is an intersection operation that returns the cell(s) that are shared by the two references you give. For example, if you have a list of items in column A and some related data in other columns, you may use a formula like this to find a value at the intersection of a certain column and row.

Example: The formula =A3:C3 C2:C4 will give you $10.000,00 in the table below.

	A	B	C	D	E
1	MONTH	BEST COUNTRY	SALES		$10.000,00	←— =A3:C3 C2:C4
2	JAN	USA	$23.000,00		
3	FEB	Italy	$10.000,00		
4	MARCH	England	$16.000,00		
5	JAN	France	$8.000,00		
6	MAR	USA	$15.000,00		

Excel Operator Order Precedence

When you write a formula with two or more separate operators, this is known as operator precedence. As a consequence, one of the operators takes priority over another or is performed first.

Example: Let's consider the formula in Excel:

=10+5*2

You may believe that the answer to this math is 30, which is 10 plus 5 multiplied by 2. Due to Operator Preference, the solution is 5 multiplied by 2 plus 10. That is why, when you input the above formula into Excel, the output is 20.

To correctly insert the formula, you would need to enter it always with brackets containing the part of the formula you want Excel to calculate first. The following formula will give you 30 as a result:

= (10+5)*2

The following is a list of all operators in ascending order of precedence.

Operator	Operation	Order of Precedence
:	Range	1st
<space>	Intersection	2nd
,	Union	3rd
–	Negation	4th
%	Percentage	5th
^	Exponentiation	6th
* and /	Multiplication and division	7th
+ and –	Addition and subtraction	8th
&	Concatenation	9th
= < > <= >= <>	Comparison	10th

Converting A Formula To A Value

Excel has the option of converting a common overused unchanged formula into a value to speed up the rate of recalculations and free up the worksheet's memory. For example, you may have formulas in part of your worksheet that uses values from a previous fiscal year. Because these numbers aren't likely to change, you can safely convert the formulas into their values. Use the following steps to convert a formula to a value:

Select the cell containing the formula.

Double-click the cell or press F2 to activate in-cell editing.

Press F9 to change the formula to its value.

Press Enter. Excel changes the cell to the value.

Additionally, you may need to replace the results of a formula in several places. For example, if a formula is in cell C4, you can display its results in other cells by entering =C4 in each of the cells. Excel will update the results of these cells and automatically update them if manual calculations are disabled. Follow the following steps to do this:

Select the cell containing the formula.

Copy the cell.

Choose the cell or cells you need to duplicate the value to.

Select *Home*, display the *Paste* list, and then select *Paste Values*. Excel will paste the selected cell's values.

The 7 Most Common Errors In Formulas And Functions

Working with Excel functions and formulas may be challenging and time-consuming, particularly when the formula or function produces an error in value rather than what you expected.

Let's have a look at the most common 7 errors that can occur while working with your functions and formulas and the reason behind them.

#DIV/0!

This indicates that the formula is trying to divide a number by zero, which is mathematically impossible. This may also happen when attempting to divide an empty cell by zero.

#NAME?

This means that Excel doesn't recognize the name given in a formula as a valid entity. This error may happen due to incorrect spelling of a function, cell reference, sheet name, or any other syntax problem.

#N/A:

This indicates that the formula is unable to produce a valid or authentic result. This happens when you use an inappropriate argument in a function. This may also happen if the lookup function does not find a match.

#NULL!

This indicates that the formula contains an intersection of two unrelated or non-interactive ranges.

#NUM!

This indicates that there is an issue with a number in your formula. Often is an incorrect argument in trig or math function.

#REF!

This indicates that the formula has an invalid cell reference, which may happen when a column or row to which the formula refers is removed. It can happen as well when the formula contains a cell reference that doesn't exist.

#VALUE

This indicates that your formula is trying to work on incorrect data.

CHAPTER 11: RELATIVE AND ABSOLUTE CELL REFERENCES IN FORMULAS

What is an Excel cell reference?

In Excel, a cell address serves as a pointer to a specific cell on a workbook. The location where to get the value you need for the calculation in Microsoft Excel.

To duplicate a cell's value to another, use the formula =A1 in cell C1. Excel will then copy the value to cell C1 from cell A1:

The same effect may be achieved by utilizing any reference type, including or excluding the dollar sign ($), in a single cell's formula:

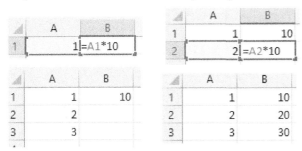

While moving or copying an equation across a spreadsheet is possible, choosing the correct reference type is vital to guarantee that the formula is copied correctly to other cells. Each cell reference type is explained and shown in depth in the following sections.

Note. Additionally, the A1 reference style, The R1C1 reference style, uses numbers to define columns and rows.

This article will cover A1-style references since they're the most often used in Excel. As a result of selecting File > Options > Formulas and then deselecting the R1C1 referencing style box, you may deactivate the R1C1 style.

Using Excel's relative cell reference

Remove the dollar sign from the cell address in the columns and rows in Excel to utilize a comparative reference, like in A1.

It is possible to copy a formula that uses relative cell references and have the reference vary dependent on the relative location of columns and rows. Excel treats all locations as a relative by default. The following example explains how relative references function.

Consider the following equation in cell B1:

=A1*10

In Excel, column A implies, you like to scale each number in column A by ten; therefore, if you copy this equation to cell B2, it will be modified for row 2 (A2*10).

	A	B
1	1	=A1*10

	A	B
1	1	10
2	2	=A2*10

	A	B
1	1	10
2	2	
3	3	

	A	B
1	1	10
2	2	20
3	3	30

A dependent cell reference in a formula will automatically change the column reference if copied:

	A	B	C
1	1	10	=B1*10
2	2	20	
3	3	30	

	A	B	C
1	1	10	100
2	2	20	200
3	3	30	300

You may also modify the column and row references of an Excel formula by copying or moving it to a new location:

	A	B
1	1	=A1*10
2	2	20
3	3	30

	A	B	C
1	1	10	
2	2	20	
3	3	30	300

When performing the exact computations over several cells on a single worksheet, utilizing relative cell references in Excel formulae is a tremendously time-saving technique. Let's take a look at a real-world scenario to understand this better.

Excel's formula example for using relative reference

To convert a column of prices (column B) from USD to EUR, you would use the following formula:

Row 2's calculation is as easy as =B2*0.93 if you know the current USD/EUR exchange rate. Use Excel's relative cell reference, which does not include a dollar sign.

When you press the Enter key, the formula is run, and the result is instantly shown in the cell.

	A	B	C
1	Item	Price, USD	Price, EUR
2	Apples	$3,00	=B2*0,93
3	Lemons	$2,00	
4	pears	$2,50	

	A	B	C
1	Item	Price, USD	Price, EUR
2	Apples	$3,00	2,79 €
3	Lemons	$2,00	
4	pears	$2,50	

Tip. Excel's default cell references are relative. Since this is a formula, click on the cell where the formula should appear, rather than manually type in a cell reference.

You may copy the formula along the column by clicking the fill handle. When you move the pointer over the cells, you want to auto-fill, a thin black cross appears.

	A	B	C
1	Item	Price, USD	Price, EUR
2	Apples	$3,00	2,79 €
3	Lemons	$2,00	
4	pears	$2,50	

Hold and drag over the cells to which you want to copy the formula.

Done! Relative references are employed for each cell in the formula to all cells. Each cell's formula may be checked by selecting and seeing the formula bar's formula. C4 has been selected as the cell reference, and the formula is based on the fourth row, as expected:

	A	B	C
1	Item	Price, USD	Price, EUR
2	Apples	$3,00	2,79 €
3	Lemons	$2,00	1,86 €
4	pears	$2,50	2,33 €

Excel cell reference with the dollar symbol ($)

An absolute reference is made using the dollar sign ($) in a column or row coordinates, as $A$1 in Excel.

The $ sign ensures that the formula's reference to a specific cell will not change, no matter where it is placed. Otherwise known as "copying without altering references," the use of $ as a cell reference enables you to do just that.

$A$1

Locks column   Locks row

For example, when you put 10 in cell A1 and apply an absolute cell reference ($A$1), the equation =$A$1+5 will produce 15. Conversely, the formula will provide different results for each row if you replicate it down to other cells in the column using a relative cell reference (A1). The change may be seen in the following photograph:

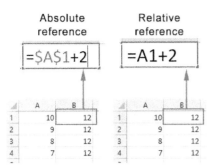

Note. Although an absolute reference in Excel doesn't ever change, when you insert or delete rows or columns from your spreadsheet, the location of the referred cell changes. A new row may be added at the top of the worksheet, and if we alter the formula to reflect that, Excel will do so:

Excel formulas that employ solely absolute references are very uncommon in real-world workbooks. However, many occupations need relative and absolute references, as seen in the examples below.

Combining a formula with both relative and absolute cell references

When replicated, it is common to require an equation that modifies cell references for rows and columns while others remain fixed on specific cells. This is a relatively common need. For example, use both absolute and relative cell references in the same calculation.

Example 1. Calculation of numbers using absolute and relative cell references

Hard-coding the currency rate isn't necessary in the previous example with USD and EUR values. As an alternative, you may insert the value in question in a different cell, such as C1, and then use the dollar symbol ($) in the formula to fix the cell reference:

	A	B	C
1	Exchange rate		0,93
2			
3	Item	Price, USD	Price, EUR
4	Apples	$3,00	=B4*$C$1
5	Lemons	$2,00	1,86 €
6	pears	$2,50	2,33 €

There are two distinct sorts of cell references in this formula (B4*$C$1):

- For each row, B4 refers to a particular cell.
- $C$1: A cell location is always the same, no matter where the formula is pasted.

This solution has the benefit of allowing your users to utilize a fluctuating exchange rate to generate EUR pricing without altering the calculation. Cell C1 may be updated to reflect any changes in the conversion rate at any time.

Example 2. Calculating dates with absolute and relative cell references

Calculating dates in Excel depending on the current date is another widespread usage of absolute and relative cell locations in an only calculation.

Consider the following scenario: you have a column B with a list of delivery dates and use the =TODAY() equation to put the current date in column C1.

When determining how many days it will take for each item to arrive, use the formula below: =B4-$C$1

	A	B	C
1	Today's date		17-nov-15
2			
3	Item	Delivery date	Ships in N days
4	Apples	17-nov-15	=B4-$C$1
5	Lemons	18-nov-15	1
6	pears	19-nov-15	2

In the formula, we employ two different sorts of references:

This cell reference should change based on which row the formula is on; therefore, it should be relative to the cell with the initial delivery date (B4).

Your current date (C$1) should be referenced as absolute because you want this cell's value to remain consistent.

The dollar sign ($) must be used in your formula to establish an Excel absolute reference when you want to construct a static cell.

Cell references in Excel that are mixed up

The column letter or the row number of a mixed cell reference in Excel is fixed. As an example, the reference $A1 and A$1 are intermingled. But what does each one mean? It couldn't be easier.

Both columns and rows are secured because of the two-dollar signs ($) in an Excel absolute reference. One of the coordinates (absolute) in a mixed cell reference is constant while the other (relative) moves about the row or column it refers to:

Relative row and absolute column, Like $A1. Using the $ sign before a column letter secures the reference to the given column, preventing it from changing even if the formula with this reference type is copied to other cells. A relative row reference without a dollar sign varies depending on the row the formula is copied.

Absolute row and Relative column, Like A$1. The reference to the row does not change when using this form of reference, but the reference to the column does.

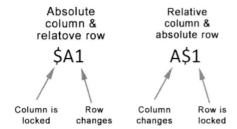

This example uses two mixed cell reference formats to help clarify. This should help.

Excel formula example of using a mixed reference

We'll use our currency exchange table once again in this case. But this time, we're not going to stop at only USD to EUR. We will use a single formula to convert dollar pricing to various monetary units.

Let's begin with the conversion rates in row 2, as indicated in the picture below. This is done by writing a single formula in the top-left cell to compute the price of the EUR:

=$B5*C$2

Where C$2 is the USD-EUR exchange rate, and $B5 is the USD rate in the same column.

	A	B	C	D	E
1	Exchange rate		USD-EUR	USD-GBP	USD-RUB
2			0,93	0,66	64,74
3					
4	Item	Price, USD	Price, EUR	Price, GBP	Price, RUB
5	Apples	$3,00	=$B5*C$2		
6	Lemons	$2,00	1,86 €		
7	pears	$2,50	2,33 €		

Using the fill handle, copy and paste the formula into extra cells in column C, and then drag it to apply the same formula to other columns. Row 2's matching exchange rate in the same column will create three pricing columns. Select any table cell and look at the formula bar formula to be sure.

Cell D7, for instance, may be used as an example (in the GBP column). Formula =$B7*D$2 gets the price in B7 and multiplies it by D2, which is the USD-GBP exchange rate, precisely what you need to get your money back.

	A	B	C	D	E
1	Exchange rate		USD-EUR	USD-GBP	USD-RUB
2			0,93	0,66	64,74
3					
4	Item	Price, USD	Price, EUR	Price, GBP	Price, RUB
5	Apples	$3,00	2,79 €	£1,98	
6	Lemons	$2,00	1,86 €	=$B6*D$2	
7	pears	$2,50	2,33 €	£1,65	

Now, let's see how Excel knows precisely what price to take and what exchange rate to multiply it by. The mixed cell references ($B5*C$2) are what do the trick.

$B5 is a column and a row that are absolute and relative, respectively. The dollar sign ($) is used solely before the column letter to ensure that Excel always utilizes the original USD pricing for all conversions in this case. Because you wish to compute the pricing for each row independently, the row reference (without the $ symbol) is not locked.

To prevent unauthorized access to the data in row 2, you must enclose the row reference with a dollar symbol ($). Once you've copied the formula to any row, Excel will always check row 2 for the current exchange rate. Because the column reference is relative (does not include the dollar sign), the calculation will be updated for the new column.

In Excel, how can you refer to a whole column or row?

Using a variable number of rows in an Excel spreadsheet may need a reference to all of the cells in a given column. There is an easier way of making a full-column reference by using A:A instead of only the first letter of the column.

A reference to an entire column

In addition to cell references, a whole column reference might be either absolute or relative:

- $A:$A is an absolute column reference.
- A:A is a column reference that is relative to another column.

In an absolute column reference, the dollar sign ($) locks the formula to a specific column so that copying it to new cells does not change the entire-column reference.

It's possible to duplicate a formula from one column to another; however, the relative column reference changes if you copy the formula to cells in the same column.

A reference to the whole row

You use the same method to refer to the complete row, only you write row numbers instead of column letters:

- $1:$1 is an absolute row reference.
- Row reference that is relative to another row, such as 1:1.

A mixed entire-column or entire-row reference, such $A:A or $1:1, is theoretically possible. In theory, I can't see any practical application for such references, even though Example 4 demonstrates that formulae containing such references operate as they should.

Entire-column reference in Excel (relative and absolute)

Assume you have countless numbers in column B and add them up. Because the database is updated weekly, utilizing SUM() or AVERAGE() for a fixed range of cells is not an option. Instead, you may use the complete column B as a reference:

= SUM($B:$B): To lock the computation to column B, creates an absolute whole-column reference ($).

= SUM(B:B): To generate a relative whole-column reference that changes when copied to other columns.

Tip. When writing the formula, click the column letter to add the entire-column reference. Standard Excel reference (no $ sign), just as it does with cell references:

	A	B	C	D	E	F	G	H
1	Item	Price, USD	Price, EUR	Price, GBP		Total, USD	Total, EUR	Total, GBP
2	Apples	$3,00	2,79 €	£1,98		=SUM(B:B)		
3	Lemons	$2,00	1,86 €	£1,32				
4	pears	$2,50	2,33 €	£1,65				

Similarly, we devise a formula to determine the column B average price:

=AVERAGE(B:B)

We're using a relative entire-column reference in this example to ensure that our formula is appropriately modified when we duplicate it to additional columns:

=AVERAGE(B:B) =AVERAGE(C:C) =AVERAGE(D:D)

	A	B	C	D	E	F	G	H
1	Item	Price, USD	Price, EUR	Price, GBP		Total, USD	Total, EUR	Total, GBP
2	Apples	$3,00	2,79 €	£1,98		$7,50	6,98 €	£4,95
3	Lemons	$2,00	1,86 €	£1,32				
4	pears	$2,50	2,33 €	£1,65		Average, USD	Average, EUR	Average, GBP
5						2,5	2,33 €	1,65 €

Note: Never put a formula in the same column as a whole-column reference in Excel. To have the sum at the end of the same column, enter the formula =SUM(B:B) in one of column B's empty bottom cells.

Example 2. Whole-row reference in Excel (relative and absolute)

If your Excel sheet has data in rows rather than columns, you may refer to a row in your calculation. For instance, in row 2, this is how we may determine an average price:

=AVERAGE($2:$2) - The dollar symbol ($) is used to lock an absolute entire-row reference to a specified row.

=AVERAGE(2:2) - The relative entire-row reference will alter when the formula is transferred to additional rows.

There are three rows of data in this example, and we need a relative reference for the entire row to calculate an average in each row using the same method:

	A	B	C	D
1	Item	Apples	Lemons	Pears
2	Price, USD	$3,00	$2,00	$2,50
3	Price, EUR	2,79 €	1,86 €	2,33 €
4	Price, GBP	£1,98	£2,33	£1,65
5				
6	Aver =AVERAGE(2:2)			
7	Average, EUR	2,33 €		
8	Average, GBP	1,65 €		

Referencing a column without the first few rows

Because many spreadsheets begin with an introduction or explanation, you do not wish to use them in your equations; this is a critical problem. Unfortunately, Excel doesn't support references like B5:B, including all of the rows in column B starting with row 5. As a result, your formula will likely produce the error message #NAME. Instead, you may provide the maximum number of rows to include in your reference, which will consist of all of the rows in that column. The maximum number of rows and columns in Excel 2021 is 1,048,576. The row and column limits in earlier versions of Excel were 65,536 for rows and 256 for columns. To calculate the average price for each column (columns B through D) in the table below, use the given formula in cell F2 and replicate it in cells G2 and H2:

=AVERAGE(B5:B1048576)

	A	B	C	D	E	F	G	H	I
1	Exchange rate		USD-EUR	USD-GBP	USD-RUB		Average, USD	Average, EUR	Average, GBP
2			0,93	0,66	64,74		=AVERAGE(B5:B1048576)	$2,33	$1,65
3							AVERAGE(number1; [number2]; ...)		
4	Item	Price, USD	Price, EUR	Price, GBP	Price, RUB				
5	Apples	$3,00	2,79 €	£1,98					
6	Lemons	$2,00	1,86 €	£1,32					
7	Pears	$2,50	2,33 €	£1,65					

It's possible to omit rows from the SUM function by using a minus sign in the SUM function:

=SUM(B:B)-SUM(B1:B4)

Example 4. A mixed reference to an entire column in Excel

In Excel, you may also add a reference to the whole column or the complete row:

- $A:A is an example of a mixed column reference
- Like $1:1, but with a mixed row reference.

Copy the formula and paste it into another cell with similar references to see what happens. For the sake of illustration, let's say you type =SUM($B:B) into cell F2. Consequently, the formula becomes =SUM($B:C) when copied to the right-hand cell (G2). Therefore, the formula will add all of the values in columns B and C. However, it's possible that you'd be interested in learning how it works:

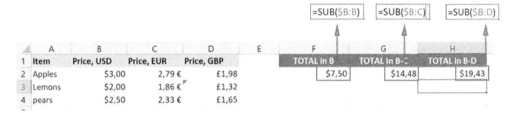

As a precautionary measure! Excel will run more slowly if there are too many references to whole columns or rows in a spreadsheet.

How to change the reference type between absolute, relative, and mixed (F4 key)

Using the $ sign in an Excel calculation to change a relative cell reference into an absolute or mixed one may be done manually. The F4 key may be used to expedite the process. To utilize the F4 shortcut, you should be in formula editing mode:

- Click the formula cell in the spreadsheet.
- Entering edit mode is as simple as pressing F2 or clicking twice on a cell.
- Change the cell reference by clicking on the desired cell.
- To switch between four different sorts of cell references, press F4.

Using the F4 key repeatedly toggles between an absolute cell reference with both dollar signs like $A$1, the absolute row A$1, and the absolute column $A1, and then back to the relative reference A1.

=A1 ⟶ =$A$1 ⟶ =A$1 ⟶ =$A1

Note. By pressing F4 without choosing a cell reference, the reference to the left of the mouse pointer is selected and altered.

We'll learn more about Excel cell references in the following sections, including referring to another worksheet, using 3D references, using structured references, and more. To wrap things up, grateful to you for reading, and I hope to see you back on our website next week!

CHAPTER 12: MUST KNOW FUNCTIONS

5 Essential Excel Functions For Beginners

THE SUM FUNCTION

The SUM function is a function that adds up values in a given cell as multiple arguments. This function is commonly used in Excel.

The SUM function uses the following arguments

=SUM (number1, [number2], [number3]......)

- Number1(Required Argument): This is the first value to sum

- Number2 (Optional Argument): This is the second value to sum

- Number3 (Optional Argument): This is the third value to sum

Practical example

With the table, let's calculate the sum of the sales made from Monday to Friday using the SUM function

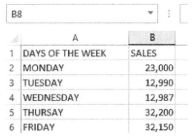

Follow the procedure below to calculate the sales from Monday to Friday using SUM:

Type the function in an empty cell with the cell range to be summed up; =SUM (A2:B6)

The total sales from Monday to Friday will be 113327

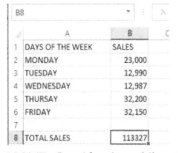

NOTE: Consider that while using the SUM function:

- The arguments provided can be constants, ranges, named ranges, or cell references. Any argument that contains errors is returned as an error by the SUM function.

- #VALUE! The error occurs when the criteria supplied are more than 255 characters long.

- SUM function ignores empty cells and cells with text values automatically

THE AVERAGE FUNCTION

It's used to calculate the average (arithmetic mean) of an arguments group. The AVERAGE function discards logical values, empty cells, and text-filled cells, and it can work with up to 255 unique parameters (including ranges, cell references, constants, and arrays).

This function uses the following arguments:

- Required Argument: First number of a cell reference or range for which the average is required.

- Optional Argument: Cell references, extra numbers, or ranges for which the average should be calculated (max, can be entered 255 characters)

Practical example

Let's have a look at how we can calculate the average of goods sold in the example below.

Select an empty cell, for example, the B6, and enter the function name and the arguments; =AVERAGE(B2:B5).

Press *Enter* so you will obtain 560.25.

NOTE: Consider that while using the AVERAGE function:

- logical values, empty cells, and cell reference argument that contains text is ignored.

- Cells having a value of zero are always counted.

- There must be only numbers inside the cells to be considered.

THE MIN FUNCTION

This function gives you the smallest or minimum number of selected values. The MIN function ignores logical values, texts, and text values.

This function needs the following argument:

=MIN (num.1, [num.2], etc.)

- Num.1, the Required Argument: Range of cells from which the lowest number will be returned.

- Num.2, the Optional Argument: Maximum 255 numbers.

Practical example

Let's say we want to find the minimum number of scores in the table below

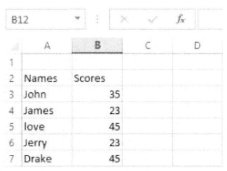

Select an empty cell, B8, for example, and enter the function name and the arguments; =MIN(B3:B7).

Press the Enter key, and you will obtain 23, the number of the minimum score.

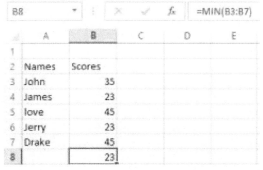

NOTE: Consider that when you select values that are not a number in the MIN function, you will be shown the VALUE! Error.

The arguments can be numbers or names, arrays or references to cells that contain numbers. In fact, logical values, empty cells, or text are not considered.

The MIN function returns 0, for any value that does not include any numbers.

THE MAX FUNCTION

This function gives you the largest or maximum number of selected values. The MAX function ignores logical values, texts, and text values.

This function needs the following argument:

=MAX(num.1, [num.2],....)

- Num.1, the Required Argument: This is the range of cells from which the highest number will be returned.

- Num.2, the Optional Argument: Maximum 255 numbers.

Practical example

Let's consider the table below. We want now find the maximum score number between those ones listed.

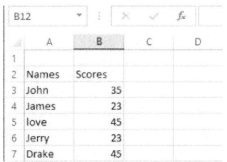

Select an empty cell, B8 as in our example, and enter the function name and the arguments; =MAX(B3:B7).

Press the Enter key, and you will obtain 45, the number of the maximum score.

B8				f_x	=MAX(B3:B7)	

	A	B	C	D	E
1					
2	Names	Scores			
3	John	35			
4	James	23			
5	love	45			
6	Jerry	23			
7	Drake	45			
8		45			

NOTE: Consider that while using the MAX function:

- When you select values that are not a number in the MAX function, it will be shown the VALUE! Error.

- The arguments can be numbers or names, arrays or references to cells that contain numbers. In fact, logical values, empty cells, or text are not considered.

- The MAX function returns 0, for any value that does not include any numbers.

THE COUNT FUNCTION

This function gives you the number of cells that contain numbers.

This function needs the following argument:

=COUNT(value1,value2,...)

- Num.1, the Required Argument: This is the cell range you want to count the ones with numbers in.

- Num.2, the Optional Argument: Maximum 255 items (cell references or ranges in which you want to count numbers)

Practical example

Let's count the number of cells that have a number in column B in the example below.

	A	B
1	Materials purchased	Quantiy
2	screws	300
3	nails	400
4	bolts	100
5	washers	

Select an empty cell, B8 as in our example, and enter the function name and the arguments; =COUNT(A2:B5).

	A	B	C	D
1	Materials purchased	Quantiy		
2	screws	300		
3	nails	400		
4	bolts	100		
5	washers			
6				
7				
8	NUMBERS OF CELLS THAT CONTAIN A NUMBER	=COUNT(A2:B5)		
9		COUNT(value1; [value2]; ...)		
10				

Press the Enter key, and you will obtain 3, the number of the cells that contain a number.

	A	B
1	Materials purchased	Quantiy
2	screws	300
3	nails	400
4	bolts	100
5	washers	?
6		
7		
8	NUMBERS OF CELLS THAT CONTAIN A NUMBER	3

NOTE: Consider that while using the COUNT function:

- Cells with numbers, dates, or a text representing numbers are the only ones considered a valid arguments. It does not count logical values TRUE or FALSE, and arguments with values or text errors are not considered.

- When an argument is an array or reference, only the numbers in the reference or array are counted.

11 Excel Functions To Pass To The Next Level

Concatenate

This function allows you to join two or more strings into a single one.

This function needs the following argument:

=CONCATENATE(text1, [text2], etc.)

- Text1 (required argument): This is the first thing to be added, and it might be a text value, a cell reference, or a number.

- Text2, (optional argument): This is the second item that will be connected to the first. It can be up to 255 items with up to 8192 characters.

Practical Example

Let's create the full name list (First Name+ Last Name) for all the football players listed below in the examples.

	A	B	C	D
1	FIRST	LAST		NAMES
2	Liam	Smith		
3	Benjamin	Johnson		
4	Oliver	Williams		
5	Noah	Brown		
6	James	Jones		
7				

Select the cell to which you want to apply the function, D2 in our example, click on the *Insert Function* button beside the Formula bar and select the function CONCAT.

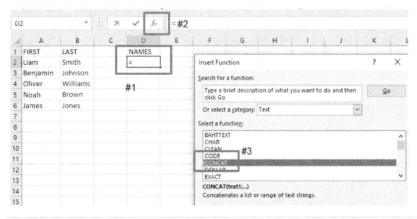

Now let's enter the Arguments.

Click on the *Text1* field and then click on the cell that *contains* the first text that you want to join (B2).

Repeat with the Text2 field, but this time typing a space, so the first text and the second one will be separated.

Click on the Text1 field and then click on the cell that contains the second name that you want to join to the first one (A2).

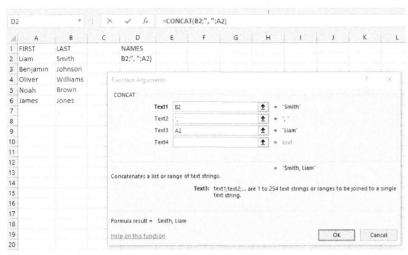

Click OK, and here below is what you will obtain.

Excel has combined the last and first name of our list.

	A	B	C	D
1	FIRST	LAST		NAMES
2	Liam	Smith		Smith, Liam
3	Benjamin	Johnson		
4	Oliver	Williams		
5	Noah	Brown		
6	James	Jones		

Select now the D2 cell and drag your mouse to the right bottom; you will see the plus sign (+); left-click on it and drag up to the last cells.

	A	B	C	D
1	FIRST	LAST		NAMES
2	Liam	Smith		Smith, Liam
3	Benjamin	Johnson		
4	Oliver	Williams		
5	Noah	Brown		
6	James	Jones		

Excell will join the names automatically, repeating the formula in the cells below

	A	B	C	D	E
1	FIRST	LAST		NAMES	
2	Liam	Smith		Smith, Liam	
3	Benjamin	Johnson		Johnson, Benjamin	
4	Oliver	Williams		Williams, Oliver	
5	Noah	Brown		Brown, Noah	
6	James	Jones		Jones, James	

VLOOKUP

This function allows you to look up and retrieve data from a specific column in the table.

This function needs the following argument:

=VLOOKUP (lookup_value, table_array, col_index_num, [range_lookup])

- Lookup_value (required argument): This is the value to search for in the table's or dataset's first column.

- Table_array (required argument): This is the data array that will be searched by the lookup value on the column's left side.

- Col_index_num (required argument): This is the table array column number or integer where the matched value must be returned.

- Range_lookup (optional argument): This portion of the function defines whether you want the VLOOK to look for an exact match or an appropriate match. The value of the argument is either TRUE or FALSE. TRUE indicates an appropriate match, and if one cannot be found, the next largest value is returned. FALSE denotes an exact match, and if one is not found, it gives the error #N/A.

Practical Example

Here below, we have a table of dates with some orders information. Let's locate a product based on a particular Order ID value in the example below.

	A	B
1	Order ID	Product
2	20350	Oranges
3	20450	Apples
4	20740	Bananas

Select an empty cell where you want to have your function result, D2 in our example, and enter the VLOOKUP function and its arguments =VLOOKUP(A3;A1:B4;2;FALSE)

CONCAT			× ✓ fx	=VLOOKUP(A3;A1:B4;2;FALSE)			
	A	B	C	D	E	F	G
1	Order ID	Product					
2	20350	Oranges		=VLOOKUP(A3;A1:B4;2;FALSE)			
3	20450	Apples					
4	20740	Bananas					

Press the Enter key, and you will obtain the Apples.

	A	B	C	D
1	Order ID	Product		
2	20350	Oranges		Apples
3	20450	Apples		
4	20740	Bananas		

INDEX MATCH

This is a more advanced version of the VLOOKUP formula (which has a number of flaws and limitations). INDEX MATCH job is to search through a large number of cells for a match. The difference with VLOOKUP function is that it returns a row or column number rather than the value of a cell.

This function needs the following argument:

=INDEX (array, row_num, [col_num]

- Array (required argument): This is the array or range of cells from which to search for information.

- Row_num (required argument): This specifies the row number of the supplied array from which a value should be returned. When this parameter is set to zero or blank, all rows in the array will be zero or blank by default.

- Column_num (optional argument): This specifies the row number of the specified array from which to return a value. When this parameter is set to zero or blank, all columns in the array default to zero or blank.

Practical Example

Let's consider the same example we used for the VLOOKUP. Now let's say that we want to know in which row the Order ID 20450 is

	A	B
1	Order ID	Product
2	20350	Oranges
3	20450	Apples
4	20740	Bananas

Select an empty cell where you want to have your function result, D3 in our example, and enter the INDEX MATCH function and its arguments =MATCH(20350; A1:A4;0).

	A	B	C	D	E	F	G	H
1	Order ID	Product						
2	20350	Oranges						
3	20450	Apples		=MATCH(20350; A1:A4;0)				
4	20740	Bananas		MATCH(lookup_value; lookup_array; [match_type])				
5								

Press the Enter key, and you will obtain 2, which is the second row on column A.

	A	B	C	D
1	Order ID	Product		
2	20350	Oranges		
3	20450	Apples		2
4	20740	Bananas		

NOTE: Consider that while using the INDEX MATCH function:

- 2 is not the second row of the sheet, but it's relative to the lookup array, so in our example, the Order ID 20450 is in the second row of the array selected.

IF

In Excel, the IF function conducts a logical comparison of two data. The IF function returns either TRUE or FALSE. We may, for example, see whether the value in cell B2 is higher than the value in cell A2. If this is the case, the result is TRUE; otherwise, the result is FALSE.

This function needs the following argument:

=IF (Logical_text,[Value_if_true],[Value_if_false])

- Logical_text (required argument): Logical expression or value that will be analyzed and determined to be TRUE or FALSE.

- Value_if_true (optional argument): If the logical test produces TRUE, this is the result that will be returned.

- Value_if_false (optional argument): If the logical test produces FALSE, this is the result that will be returned.

With this function, you will use the following operators: *Equal to* ($=$), *Greater than* ($>$), *Greater than or equal to* ($\geq$), *Less than* ($<$), *Less than or equal to* ($\leq$), *Not equal* ($\neq$).

Practical Example

Considering the quantities of the products shown in the example below, we want the IF function to return a value "Reorder" if the quantity of the products is less than 15.

	A	B
1	Product	Quantity
2	Oranges	8
3	Apples	3
4	Bananas	12

Select an empty cell where you want to have your function result, D2 in our example, and enter the IF function and its arguments =IF(B2<15;"Reorder")

	A	B	C	D	E	F	G
1	Product	Quantity					
2	Oranges	8		=IF(B2<15;"Reorder")			
3	Apples	3		IF(logical_test; [value_if_true]; [value_if_false])			
4	Bananas	12					

Press the Enter key, and you should see the value "Reorder" appear in cell D3 since the value contained in cell B3 is 3, which is less than 15.

	A	B	C	D
1	Product	Quantity		
2	Oranges	8		Reorder
3	Apples	3		
4	Bananas	12		

Now let's copy the formula in D3 and D4.

Select now the D2 cell and drag your mouse to the right bottom; you will see the plus sign (+); left-click on it and drag up to the last cells.

	A	B	C	D
1	Product	Quantity		
2	Oranges	8		Reorder
3	Apples	3		
4	Bananas	12		
5				

The result will be as shown below.

Excel has returned the value "Reorder" as the quantities of Apples and Bananas are less than 15.

	A	B	C	D
1	Product	Quantity		
2	Oranges	8		Reorder
3	Apples	3		Reorder
4	Bananas	12		Reorder

Here below, you can see the result if, for example, the apple quantities were greater than 15.

	A	B	C	D
1	Product	Quantity		
2	Oranges	8		Reorder
3	Apples	25		FALSE
4	Bananas	12		Reorder

Notice that in cell D3 the value FALSE appears. Since we didn't specify the third parameter in our formula, the IF function will return FALSE when the condition evaluates to FALSE

Let's say now that, instead of FALSE, we want to have a blank value when the condition evaluates FALSE. We would need to enter the third value, and the following will be our function with its arguments

=IF(B2<15;"Reorder";"")

This time we are entering 2 quotation marks ("") as a third parameter, which represents a blank value or empty string. See below the result.

	A	B	C	D
1	Product	Quantity		
2	Oranges	8		Reorder
3	Apples	25		
4	Bananas	12		Reorder

CHOOSE

The CHOOSE function is great for analyzing financial simulation scenarios. It allows you to return the value from a list of values based on its position in the list

This function uses an index number provided to return a value from the list of value arguments.

Choose function needs the following argument:

=CHOOSE (index_num, value1, [value2] …)

- Index_num (required argument): This is an integer that specifies the position of the value to return. This must contain any number between 1 and 254, a formula, or a reference to a cell ranging between 1 and 254

- Value1, Value2, ValueXThis is a list that ranges from 1 and 254 values from which the CHOOSE function is to look from. The value 1 is required, while others are optional. These values can come in the form of numbers, text values, formulas, cell references, or defined names.

Practical Example

Consider the player's list below. We want the CHOOSE function to return the name of a team drawn.

	A	B	C
1	Players		Random pick
2	Mike		Winner
3	Liam		
4	Diego		
5	Amy		

Select the cell where you want to have your function result, D3 in our example, and enter the CHOOSE function and its arguments = =CHOOSE(D2;A3;A4;A5)

D2 is the cell to enter the random pick number.

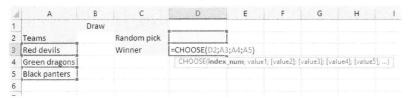

Press the Enter key. You should now see the error #VALUE! because we still have to enter a number in the cell D2.

	A	B	C	D
1		Draw		
2	Teams		Random pick	
3	Red devils		Winner	#VALUE!
4	Green dragons			
5	Black panters			

Try to enter 2, for example, and in cell D2 it will be returned the second value of our list, which is Green Dragons.

	A	B	C	D
1		Draw		
2	Teams		Random pick	2
3	Red devils		Winner	Green dragons
4	Green dragons			
5	Black panters			

COUNTIF

The COUNTIF function is used to count the number of cells that meet a certain criterion or condition. The cells could contain dates, numbers, and text. This function also supports the use of logical operators and wildcards.

This function needs the following argument:

=COUNTIF(Range; "criteria")

- Range (required argument): This indicates the range of cells that have to be counted.

- Criteria (required argument): This is the condition to be met by the cells provided with the range. The criteria argument could be:

- A numerical value (decimal, integer, decimal, logical value, or time)

- A text string (East, Monday, East, and including wildcards such as asterisks and question marks)

Practical Example

With the table below, let's use the COUNTIF function to count how many times Mike's name appears on the list.

	A	B
1	Year	Winner
2	2015	Mike
3	2016	James
4	2017	Oliver
5	2018	Noah
6	2019	Mike
7	2020	Mike
8	2021	oliver

Select an empty cell, type in the function name and the arguments to be used; =COUNTIF(B2:B6, "James").

Select a cell where you want to have your function result, D2 in our example, and enter the COUNTIF function and the arguments =COUNTIF(B2:B8;"mike").

	A	B	C	D	E	F
1	Year	Winner				
2	2015	Mike		=COUNTIF(B2:B8;"mike")		
3	2016	James				
4	2017	Oliver				
5	2018	Noah				
6	2019	Mike				
7	2020	Mike				
8	2021	oliver				

Click on Enter, and the result will be 3

	A	B	C	D
1	Year	Winner		
2	2015	Mike		3
3	2016	James		
4	2017	Oliver		
5	2018	Noah		
6	2019	Mike		
7	2020	Mike		
8	2021	oliver		

NOTE: Consider that while using the COUNTIF function:

- The criteria argument is always enclosed in quotes, e.g., "mike."

- When the provided criteria argument is a text with more than 255 characters, it will be shown the #VALUE error.

- #VALUE error occurs when the formula is referring to a cell or range of cells in a closed workbook

THE SUMIF FUNCTION

The SUM function is one that sums up cells based on the criteria or conditions provided. The Criteria or conditions are based on dates, numbers, and texts. This function makes use of logical operators such as <, >, etc. and wildcats (*,?)

This function needs the following argument:

=SUMIF (range, criteria, [sum_range]

- Range (required argument): Cells range that the criteria are applied against

- Criteria (required argument): This is what determines the cells to be summed up. The criteria argument could be:

- A numerical value (decimal, integer, decimal, logical value, or time)

- A text string (East, Monday, East, and including wildcards such as asterisks and question marks)

- An expression e.g. >11, <3 etc.

- Sum_range (optional argument): This is the cell to sum up, if there are other cells, to sum up apart from the ones specified in the range argument

Practical Example

To have a clear picture of how the SUMIF function is used, let's calculate the sales made in December only in the USA.

	A	B	C
1	MONTH	BEST COUNTRY	SALES
2	JAN	USA	$23.000,00
3	FEB	Italy	$10.000,00
4	MARCH	England	$16.000,00
5	JAN	France	$8.000,00
6	MAR	USA	$15.000,00
7	MARCH	USA	$7.000,00
8	JAN	USA	$3.000,00
9	ABR	Italy	$8.700,00
10	MARCH	France	$6.500,00
11	JAN	Germany	$5.000,00
12	MAY	USA	$3.400,00

First thing, let's calculate the total sales made in Jan. Enter the SUMIF function with its arguments =SUMIF(A2:A12;"jan";C2:C12)

	A	B	C	D
1	MONTH	BEST COUNTRY	SALES	
2	JAN	USA	$23.000,00	
3	FEB	Italy	$10.000,00	
4	MARCH	England	$16.000,00	
5	JAN	France	$8.000,00	
6	MAR	USA	$15.000,00	
7	MARCH	USA	$7.000,00	
8	JAN	USA	$3.000,00	
9	ABR	Italy	$8.700,00	
10	MARCH	France	$6.500,00	
11	JAN	Germany	$5.000,00	
12	MAY	USA	$3.400,00	
13				
14	TOT Sales for JAN	=SUMIF(A2:A12;"jan";C2:C12)		
15		SUMIF(range; criteria; [sum_range])		

The total sale of Jan is $39.000,00, and it is shown in the table below

	A	B	C
1	MONTH	BEST COUNTRY	SALES
2	JAN	USA	$23.000,00
3	FEB	Italy	$10.000,00
4	MARCH	England	$16.000,00
5	JAN	France	$8.000,00
6	MAR	USA	$15.000,00
7	MARCH	USA	$7.000,00
8	JAN	USA	$3.000,00
9	ABR	Italy	$8.700,00
10	MARCH	France	$6.500,00
11	JAN	Germany	$5.000,00
12	MAY	USA	$3.400,00
13			
14	TOT Sales for JAN	$39.000,00	

Now, we want the total sales made in the USA.

Let's type in a new cell the function and the arguments =SUMIF(B2:B12;"usa";C2:C12)

	A	B	C
1	MONTH	BEST COUNTRY	SALES
2	JAN	USA	$23.000,00
3	FEB	Italy	$10.000,00
4	MARCH	England	$16.000,00
5	JAN	France	$8.000,00
6	MAR	USA	$15.000,00
7	MARCH	USA	$7.000,00
8	JAN	USA	$3.000,00
9	ABR	Italy	$8.700,00
10	MARCH	France	$6.500,00
11	JAN	Germany	$5.000,00
12	MAY	USA	$3.400,00
13			
14	TOT Sales for JAN	$39.000,00	
15	TOT Sales in USA	=SUMIF(B2:B12;"usa";C2:C12)	

The total sales made in the USA are $51.400,00.

	A	B	C
1	MONTH	BEST COUNTRY	SALES
2	JAN	USA	$23.000,00
3	FEB	Italy	$10.000,00
4	MARCH	England	$16.000,00
5	JAN	France	$8.000,00
6	MAR	USA	$15.000,00
7	MARCH	USA	$7.000,00
8	JAN	USA	$3.000,00
9	ABR	Italy	$8.700,00
10	MARCH	France	$6.500,00
11	JAN	Germany	$5.000,00
12	MAY	USA	$3.400,00
13			
14	TOT Sales for JAN	$39.000,00	
15	TOT Sales in USA	$51.400,00	

NOTE: Consider that while using the SUMIF function:

- VALUE! The error occurs when the criteria supplied are more than 255 characters long.

- The cells in range will be summed automatically when the sum_range is omitted.

- Text strings in criteria must be enclosed in double-quotes. Otherwise, it will not work.

- You can use the wildcards " ? " and " * " can be used in the SUMIF function.

PROPER
The PROPER function is a function that changes texts or characters into a proper case. It sets the first character in each word to uppercase and the remaining letters in lowercase.

The PROPER function uses just an argument which is =PROPER(Text)

- Text (required argument): This is the text you wish to change to a proper case. It can be a text string or a cell reference

USING THE PROPER FUNCTION
Let's change the text strings in our example below to a proper case using the PROPER function.

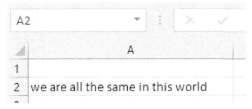

Select the cell where you want the result will be entered, and type in the function and its argument =PROPER(A2)

	A	B	C
1			
2	we are all the same in this world	=PROPER(A2)	
3			

Click on the enter key, and the text strings will be converted to a proper case, as shown here below.

	A	B	C	D	E
1					
2	we are all the same in this world	We Are All The Same In This World			

NOTE: Consider that while using the PROPER function:

- The first letter of each text string is converted to an upper case while the remaining words are changed into lower case.

- The PROPER function does not affect numbers and punctuations.

TRIM FUNCTION

The TRIM function is used to remove extra spaces from a text, leaving only a single space between words and with no space character at the start or end of the text.

This function needs the following argument:

=TRIM(text)

- Text (required argument): This is the text you wish to remove the spaces from

Practical Example

We want to remove the spaces in the texts in the table below using the TRIM function.

Choose an empty cell and type in the TRIM function and the argument

=TEXTJOIN(",", TRUE, A2, A3, A4, A5, A6).

Click the enter key, and the texts will be joined to form a single text string, as shown here below.

NOTE: Consider that while using the TRIM function:

- It only removes extra spaces from text and leaves just a single space in the texts.

- It is useful for cleaning up text that comes from other applications or environments.

- Removes the ASCII space character from the text

LEN FUNCTION

The LEN function returns the numbers of characters in a text string, excluding the number formatting.

This function needs the following argument:

=LEN(text)

- Text (Required Argument): This is the text you wish to find or calculate its length.

Practical Example

In the table below, find the numbers of characters using the LEN function.

To find the numbers of characters in the A2 cell, in or example below, just select an empty cell, B2, and enter the function with its argument =LEN(A2)

Click on enter, and the number of text strings will be 41, as shown in the table below

NOTE: Consider that while using the LEN function:

- Spaces are counted as characters.

- The number of formatting is not included.

THE LENB FUNCTION

The LENB function returns the number of bytes used in representing characters in a text string.

This function needs the following argument:

=LEN(text)

- Text (Required Argument): This is the length you wish to find or calculate the length of a text string.

Practical Example

Considering the example below, find the length of the text strings in cell A3 using the LENB function

	A	B	C	D
1				
2	Information and Communication Technology	41		
3	爱是一件美丽的事			
4				

Select an empty cell, and type in the function and its argument =LENB(A3). Click the enter key, and the number of text strings will be 8.

=LENB(A3)

	A	B	C
1			
2	Information and Communication Technology	41	
3	爱是一件美丽的事	8	
4			

NOTE: Consider that while using the LEB function:

- Spaces are counted as characters.

- The number of formatting is not included.

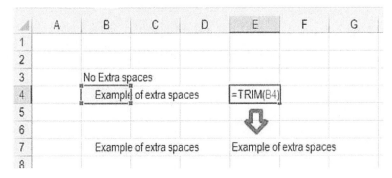

MODULE E

CHAPTER 13: DATA VALIDATION

Data validation is a spreadsheet feature that allows you to create a list of specific entries, which will then restrict what values you can place in each cell. You can also create a message elaborating on what types of data will be allowed in the cells, add a warning when the wrong type of data is put into the cells, and check for cells filled with the wrong information through the use of the Audit function. Finally, you can set a range of specific values to be placed in any cell or determine this range based on the results of a different cell.

Allow a set of values to be entered into a cell

To ensure a specific set of values are the only values that a specific cell or set of cells will accept, you must first create an acceptable list of values before setting the cell to only accept those values.

Begin by clicking on cell A1 to select it

Go to the menu labeled Data before choosing the option for Validation

Select the option for settings, then choose the list option from the dropdown menu.

Find the box labeled source, and fill it in with a,b,c before selecting the OK option. This box can also be filled with a range that has been named or a specific reference to a cell that contains a set of values listed. If you chose this option, enter = before entering the specifics.

When done correctly, A1 will now show a list that provides a list of acceptable values. What you select will then appear in the cell. Values can also be typed into the cell though only allowed numbers will be allowed to remain.

Add a message listing allowed data

After creating a message, it will appear every time you select the cell to which it is attached. This message can be moved to a new location or, if Office Assistant is active, the message will appear there instead.

Choose the cell you wish to add the message to.

Select the menu labeled Data before selecting the option labeled Validation and choosing the tab labeled Input Message.

Ensure the box indicating the message will be shown is checked

Select the box labeled Title before typing a title for your message before selecting the message box and entering your message. Ensure you click OK, or nothing will be saved.

Add a message to show when the wrong data has been entered

These messages come in two types, those which prevent the wrong type of data be added to the cell or range of cells in question and those which don't. Limits can also be set on what can be entered into the cells without any message displaying.

Choose the cell you wish to add the message to.

Select the menu labeled Data before selecting the option labeled Validation and choosing the tab labeled Error Alert.

Ensure the show alert box is checked before determining the type of message you want to set.

If you want to create the type of message that won't allow the wrong values to be added to a cell, choose the list labeled Style and select the Stop option. Add a title for the message in the box labeled title and the bulk of the message in the box labeled message. The message should list what values are allowed. Ensure you click OK, or nothing will be saved.

If you want to create a message that will warn the user of incorrect values, instead visit the Style list and choose the Warning option. This will force the user to choose to continue when incorrect values are added to specific cells. Add a title for the message in the box labeled title and the bulk of the message in the box labeled message. The message should list what values are allowed. Ensure you click OK, or nothing will be saved.

If you want to create a message that will simply inform the user of incorrect values, instead visit the Style list and choose the Inform option. Add a title for the message in the box labeled title and the bulk of the message in the box labeled message. The message should list what values are allowed. Ensure you click OK, or nothing will be saved.

Choose the list labeled Allow, and the option labeled Customize.

Select the formula box and add the following to it: =IF(cell1>cell2, TRUE, FALSE) where cell1 and cell2 are the cells you wish to relate to one another. This formula can be used with any function, not just IF; it must always contain the equal sign as well as the true and false evaluation.

Select OK to save your function.

Excel has a series of controls in place, which will help to accurately determine when specific ranges of cells are related to one another. It requires blank columns or rows in the related areas in order to work properly. Sorting can be done in numerous ways, text can be sorted alphabetically, numbers can be sorted from highest to lowest or lowest to heist, times and dates can be sorted based on age, and custom sorting includes things like cell color font size, icon and more.

Performing Data Validation In Excel

Follow the steps below to apply data validation in Excel.

Open the Data Validation dialog box. Choose one or more cells to be verified, then press the Data Validation key on the Data tab.

Alternatively, you can open a Data Validation dialog box by pressing Alt + D + L, one key at a time.

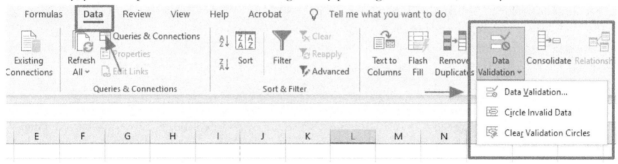

Create a validation rule. Establish the validity conditions on your Settings tab according to your values — fill in the parameter boxes with numbers, as seen in the example below.

Create a rule dependent on a formula or value in another cell using cell comparisons.

Formulas - enable the expression of more complicated situations, such as those in this example.

Let's say you choose to create a rule that only allows users to enter whole numbers between 1000 and **9999**:

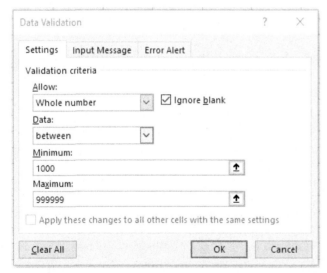

After you have configured your validation rule, press OK to close the *Data Validation* window or turn to another tab to add the input message and error warning.

Input Message

Add the input message

Fill in the appropriate fields with the title and text of the message.

To close a dialog window, click the OK button.

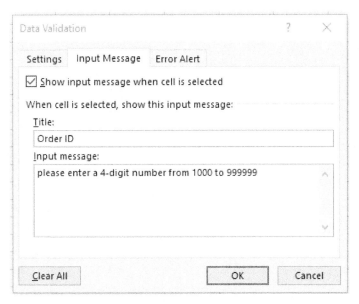

The following notification will display as soon as the user selects a validated cell:

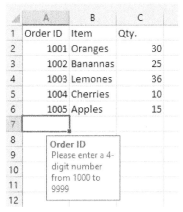

Display the error alert. If inaccurate data is inserted in the cell, you can display one of the error messages below in response to an input message.

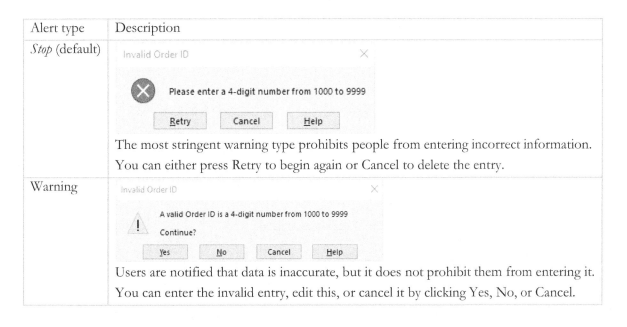

Alert type	Description
Stop (default)	The most stringent warning type prohibits people from entering incorrect information. You can either press Retry to begin again or Cancel to delete the entry.
Warning	Users are notified that data is inaccurate, but it does not prohibit them from entering it. You can enter the invalid entry, edit this, or cancel it by clicking Yes, No, or Cancel.

Information	
	The most lenient warning type informs users only of an incorrect data entry. To enter an incorrect value, press OK or cancel to delete it from a cell.

Go to the Error Alert tab and set the following parameters to create a custom error alert message: Check the box to display an error message if incorrect data is inserted (usually checked by default).

Choose the alarm type in your Style box.

In the appropriate boxes, type the text and title of the error message.

Select OK.

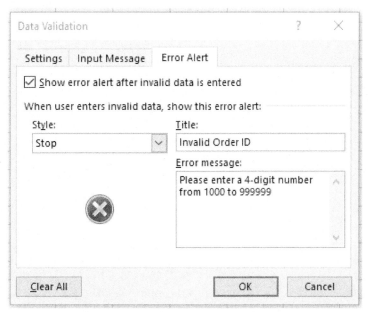

Excel will now present a special warning detailing the error if the user enters incorrect results (such as those displayed at the start of this chapter).

Note: If people don't type their message, the Stop warning appears with the following text: This value doesn't comply with the data validation rules set for this cell.

Data Validation Samples

You have the option of using one of the predefined parameters or specifying custom conditions based on the validation algorithm while applying a rule for data validation in Excel. The built-in options are discussed below, and you'll take a more in-depth look at formulas for data validation in Excel.

The validation parameters are specified on the *Settings* tab of the *Data Validation* dialog box (Data tabs / Data Validation), as you know.

Whole numbers and decimals. Select the appropriate item in the Allow box to limit data entry to decimals or whole numbers. Then, in the Data box, choose one of the following conditions:

- Is the stated amount equivalent or not equivalent to a specified number?

- The amount must be greater or less than the given value.

- To rule out a set of numbers, you can set the function to choose between two numbers or not choose between two numbers.

This is how, for instance, you can make a rule for Excel validation that requires only whole numbers greater than zero to be entered:

Date and time validation. Choose *Date* in the *Allow* box to verify times and then choose a suitable criterion in the Databox. There are also predefined options to choose from, such as allowing only dates between two fixed dates, only allowing dates that are before or after a given date, and so on. Select Time in the Allow box to verify the times and then specify the appropriate conditions. Apply this type of Excel date validity rule, for instance, to accept only dates between the *Start* date in cell B 1 and the End date in B 2:

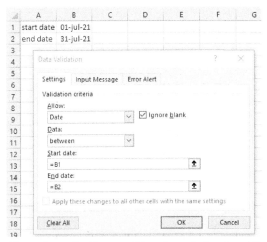

Text length. Choose Text length in the Allow box to enable data entry of a given duration and then set the validity conditions according to your requirements.

Establish this rule, for instance, to restrict the input to ten characters:

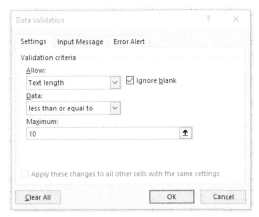

Note that the Text length option only restricts the number of characters, not your data type, so the rule above would allow all text and numbers of less than ten digits or characters.

Data validation dropdown lists in Excel. Select the desired cells and perform the following steps to apply data validation to a dropdown list of items: (Data tab☐ Data Validation) Open the Data Validation dialog window.

- Select List from the Allow dropdown menu on the Settings tab.

- Type the items from your validation list into the Source box, separated by commas. Type No, Yes, and N/A to restrict the user feedback to three options.

- To see the dropdown arrow beside the cell, ensure your In-cell dropdown box is chosen.

- Select OK.

The list of data validation results should resemble this:

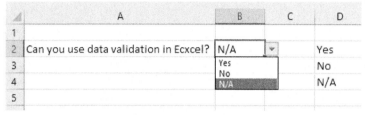

Note: An Ignore blank alternative, which is chosen by default, should be used with caution. Selecting such a check box requires you to insert a value into the validated cell while building a dropdown list centered on a specific set of nearly blank cells. It is also relevant for validation formulas in certain cases; for example, when a cell specified in a formula appears blank, any meaning can be entered in the validated cell.

Editing Data Validation

Follow these measures to modify a validation rule:

Any validated cells may be chosen.

(Data tab / Data Validation) Open the Data Validation dialog window.

Make the necessary adjustments.

To copy these changes to all cells with original validation conditions, choose the Apply the changes to all cells using the setting check box of the same name.

To save the improvements, click OK.

For example, you can adjust the items in your list of data validation by inserting or deleting them from the Source box, and the modifications will be added to other cells to produce an identical dropdown list:

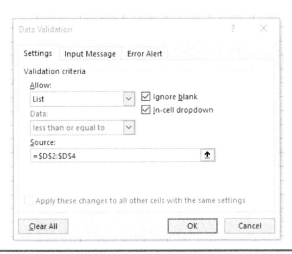

Finding Cells Using Data Validation

Go to *Home* tab / Editing / Find and Select / Data Validation to identify the validated cells in the current worksheet easily:

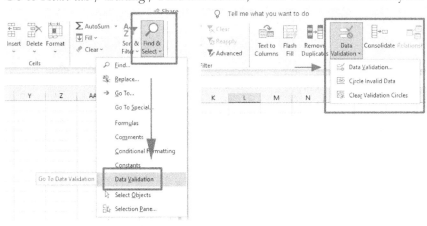

This will select all that cells that are subject to certain rules for data validation:

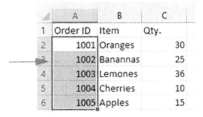

	A	B	C
1	Order ID	Item	Qty.
2	1001	Oranges	30
3	1002	Banannas	25
4	1003	Lemones	36
5	1004	Cherries	10
6	1005	Apples	15

Removing Data Validation

Method 1: *Standard method for removing data validation* To delete data validation from worksheets, the usual method is to follow these steps:

- Choose the cell(s) that contain data validation.

- Click the Data Validation icon on the Data tab.

- Click the Clear All key on your Settings tab, then click the OK key.

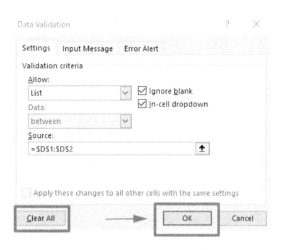

Use the Find and Select option to choose all validated cells on the current sheet to delete data validity from all of them. Select a cell with a data validation regulation, open the Data Validation dialog window, check on Apply these modifications to all cells with the same settings box, and then press the Clear All key to delete the rule. As you can see, the traditional approach is very fast, but it does necessitate some mouse clicks, which isn't a major problem for many people. However, if you choose to operate with a keyboard rather than a cursor, you might find the following method appealing. *Method 2: Paste Special to delete rules for data validation* Paste Special is intended for pasting basic elements in copied cells, according to the rule, but it's capable of a lot more. It can, for example, easily delete rules for data validation from a worksheet. Here's how to do it: Select an empty cell with no data validation and copy it using CTRL+C.

Select any cell(s) where data validation should be removed. The shortcut for the Paste Special / Data Validation is CTRL+Alt+V, then N.

Enter the code. That's it!

Copying Rule For Data Validation To Other Cells

You don't have to start again if you establish a validation rule for a cell and choose to use it to validate certain cells with the same criterion later.

Follow these four simple steps to copy a validation law in Excel:

- To copy the cells to which the validation rule refers, select them and click CTRL+C.

- Choose which other cells you'd like to verify. Click and hold the CTRL key to choose the non-adjacent cells.

- Click Validation from the context menu after right-clicking the list and selecting Paste Special. Alternatively, use CTRL+Alt+V, then N workarounds for Paste Special / Validation.

- Select OK.

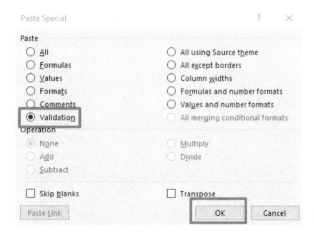

It is useful to transform a data set to a table rather than copying the data validation to other cells. Excel can automatically extend the validation rule to new rows when you add further rows to a table.

Advanced Data Validation Tricks

Now that you've learned the fundamentals of Excel data validation, a few additional hints will help you improve the effectiveness of your Excel actions.

Data validation that is dependent on another cell.

You can enter values in certain cells instead of in specific parameter sections and then apply them to other cells. You don't have to change the steps if you wish to adjust the validity criteria later as you only need to type new figures into the document.

To enter a cell connection, type this in a box followed by the equal sign or press the arrow beside the box. Then, select a cell with your mouse. You can also select a cell on a sheet by clicking anywhere inside the box. Choose the non-equal to criterion in the Data box and type = $A$1 in the Value box to accept any whole amount other than the number in A1:

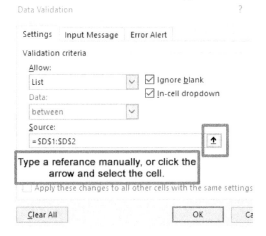

To prevent users from entering dates beyond today's date, for instance, enter the = TODAY () formula in a cell, such as B1, and then create a rule for Date validation centered upon the cell:

Alternatively, you can type the = TODAY () formula straight into the *Start* date box to achieve the same result.

Troubleshooting Data Validation in Excel

If the data validation of your worksheets isn't running correctly, it's almost certainly due to one of the following issues. Data validation doesn't work for the copied data.

In Excel, data validation prevents users from typing inaccurate data directly into cells, but this does not prevent people from copying incorrect data. Although you can't disable the copy/paste shortcuts (unless you use VBA), you can at least prevent data from being copied by dragging and dropping cells. Clear the Allow fill handle and cell drag-and-drop check box in *File* / Options / Advanced / Editing options.

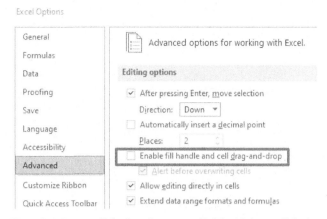

Excel's data validation is unavailable if the cell is in edit mode.

If you're entering or modifying data inside a cell, the Data Validation control is disabled (grayed out). After you have finished editing your cell, exit the edit mode by pressing Enter or Esc and then perform data validation.

Data validation does not function in a shared or protected workbook.

In secure and shared workbooks, the current validation rules are retained, so it's not feasible to modify data validation settings or create new rules. Unshare and unprotect the workbook first to do this.

Incorrect formulas for data validation.

There are three conditions to check while performing data validation (formula-based) in Excel:

- There are no flaws in the validation formula.

- An empty cell is not referred to in a formula.

- Cell references have been used appropriately.

- Please check the 'Custom data validation rule is not working' for more details.

Manual recalculation is turned on.

Uncalculated formulas will prevent data from being checked correctly if a Manual Calculation feature is activated in Excel. Go to Formulas tab / Calculation group, click the Calculation Options icon, and now click Automatic to return the Excel calculation function to automatic.

In Excel, this is how to integrate and use the data validation.

Figures in €/000: Sell-Out & Inter-CO **Intake Monthly YTD: YearMonth 202105**

Kpi Date Month	Order Intake YTD PY	Order Intake YTD CY	% Var	Qty Intake YTD PY PF	Qty Intake YTD CY PF	% Var
01	3.465,5	3.044,8	-12,1%	46.005	43.920	-4,5%
02	3.017,1	3.162,7	4,8%	45.639	46.321	1,5%
03	2.289,0	4.820,0	110,6%	35.471	61.158	72,4%
04	1.355,2	5.955,7	339,5%	15.009	79.204	427,7%
05	1.572,2	6.015,1	282,6%	18.635	87.706	370,7%
TOTAL	11.698,9	22.998,4	96,6%	160.759	318.309	98,0%

Channel Name	Kpi Date Month	Order Intake YTD PY	Order Intake YTD CY	% Var	Qty Intake YTD PY PF	Qty Intake YTD CY PF	% Var
	01	3.454,0	3.005,0	-13,0%	45.993	43.906	-4,5%
	02	3.017,1	3.155,7	4,6%	45.639	46.296	1,4%
Sell-Out	03	2.281,6	4.633,6	103,1%	35.466	60.744	71,3%
	04	1.354,1	5.754,5	325,0%	15.009	79.159	427,4%
	05	1.568,4	5.995,7	282,3%	18.632	87.597	370,1%
Sell-Out		11.675,2	22.544,4	93,1%	160.739	317.702	97,7%
	01	11,5	39,8	246,6%	12	14	16,7%
	02	0,0	7,1	100,0%	0	25	100,0%
Inter-Company	03	7,4	186,5	2.426,5%	5	414	8.180,0%
	04	1,1	201,2	17.915,1%	0	45	100,0%
	05	3,7	19,4	423,8%	3	109	3.533,3%
Inter-Company		23,7	454,0	1.815,7%	20	607	2.935,0%
TOTAL		11.698,9	22.998,4	96,6%	160.759	318.309	98,0%

... | Turnover Country YTD | Turnover Country-Customer YTD | Turnover by BU YTD | Inta

CHAPTER 14: PIVOT TABLES

Traditional Excel tables quickly hit their limits, as they are often too rigid for someone who needs to analyze large quantities of data. The best choice is to use pivot tables with advanced functionality. Pivot tables in Excel demonstrate their full potential for interpreting and preparing data, and they can be used to:

- Display enormous volumes of data in a user-friendly manner.

- Data can be summarized by categories and subcategories.

- Filter, organize, sort, and conditionally format various subsets of data to concentrate on the most important information.

- To examine multiple summaries of the source data, rotate rows to columns or columns to rows (this is known as "pivoting").

- In the spreadsheet, subtotal and aggregate numerical data.

- Expand or collapse the data layers and dive down to examine the specifics behind each total.

- Present your data or printed reports in a succinct and appealing manner online.

Create A Pivot Table

Organize your data

Organize your data into rows and columns before making a summary report, and then transform your data range into an Excel Table. To do so, select all of the data, go to the *Insert tab*, and then click *Table*. When you use an Excel Table as the source data, you get a very pleasant benefit: your data range becomes "dynamic." A dynamic range in this context indicates that your Table will automatically grow and decrease as you add or delete items, so you won't have to worry that your pivot table is out of date.

Create The pivot Table

In the source data table, select any cell. Go to the *Insert* tab on the *Tables* group, and click on *PivotTable*.

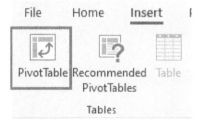

This will open the Create PivotTable Popup box. In the Table/Range field, ensure that the relevant table or range of cells is marked. Then, for your Excel pivot table, choose the following location:

When you choose New Worksheet, a table will be created in a new worksheet, beginning with cell A1.

When you choose Existing Worksheet, your table will be placed in the provided position in an existing worksheet. Click the Collapse Dialog button in the Location box. Use the Collapse Dialog button to choose the first cell in which you wish to place your table.

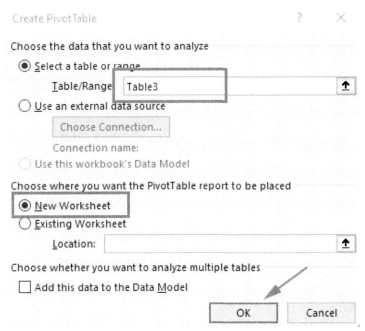

By clicking OK, you will build a blank pivot table in the desired place, which will look like this:

Please note 3 things about creating Pivot Tables:

1: In most circumstances, it is logical to put a pivot table in a separate worksheet; this is particularly important for novices.

2: If you're making a pivot table using data in another worksheet or workbook, add the workbook and worksheet names with the syntax [workbook name]. For example, [Book1] sheet name!range .xlsx]

3: Sheet1!$A$1:$E$20. Alternatively, you may use the Collapse Dialog button to close the dialog. Click the Collapse Dialog button and use the mouse to choose a table or range of cells in another worksheet.

Pivot Table Report Layout

The PivotTable Field List is the place where you deal with the fields of your summary report. It is positioned on the right side of the worksheet and is separated into two sections: the header and the body:

The Field Section lists the names of the fields you may include in your table. The names of the fields match the column names in your source table.

The Layout Section includes the Report Filter, Column Labels, Row Labels, and Values areas. You may rearrange the fields of your table in this section.

Changes made in the PivotTable Field List are instantly reflected in the table.

Adding a field to the pivot table

If you wish to add one field to the Layout section, tick the box next to its name in the Field section.

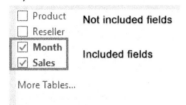

By default, Microsoft Excel adds the following fields to the Layout section:

- Row Labels now include non-numerical fields.

- Numeric fields have been added to the Values section.

- Date and time hierarchies from Online Analytical Processing (OLAP) are now available in the Column Labels section.

Remove a field from a Pivot table

To remove a specific field, you may do one of two things:

1: Uncheck the box next to the field's name in the PivotTable pane's Field section.

2: Remove the field from your pivot table by right-clicking it and selecting "Remove Field Name."

Arrange pivot table fields

You can do this in three ways:

1: Using the mouse, drag and drop fields between the four sections of the Layout section.

2: In the Field section, right-click the field name and then pick the place where you want to add it:

3: In the Layout section, click on the field to pick it. This will also reveal the alternatives for that specific field.

PivotTable Field List

The pivot table pane, previously known as the PivotTable Field List, is the primary tool for arranging your summary table precisely as you want it.

You may wish to adjust the window to your desire to make working with the fields more comfortable.

If you wish to modify the arrangement of the sections in the Field List, click the Tools icon and choose your desired layout.

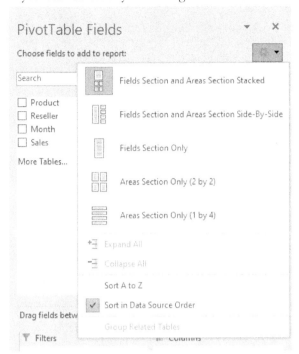

Closing the *Pivot Table Field List* is as simple as clicking the Close button (X) in the pane's upper right corner.

To re-display, the Field List, right-click anywhere in the table and choose *Show Field List* from the context menu, or by using the *Field List* button on the *Ribbon* (Show group on the Analyze / Options tab)

Work With The Pivot Table

Now that you understand the fundamentals, you may explore the groups and choices available on the PivotTable Analyze. When you click anywhere inside your table, these tabs become visible.

Improve your Pivot Table

To enhance the design of the table, go to the *Design* page, where you'll discover a plethora of pre-defined designs. Select the *More* button in the Pivot Table Styles gallery, then click "*New PivotTable Style...*" to build your own style.

To change the layout of a certain field, select it and then click the *Field Settings* button on the Analyze tab (*Active Field* group)

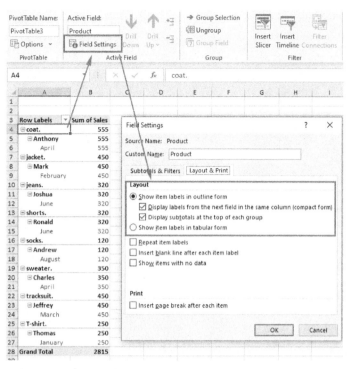

Row Labels" and "Column Labels" headings

Excel uses the Compact layout by default when generating a pivot table. The table headers in this arrangement are "*Row Labels*" and "*Column Labels*." I agree that they aren't particularly informative titles, especially for newcomers.

Switching from the *Compact style* to *Outline* or *Tabular* is a simple approach to get rid of these awful headlines. Navigate to the *Design* tab on the *Ribbon*, choose *Report Layout* from the dropdown menu, and then either *Show in Outline Form* or *Show in Tabular Form*.

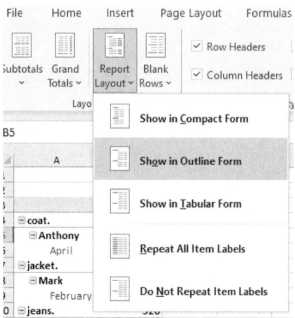

This will show the real field names, as seen in the table on the right, which makes a lot more sense.

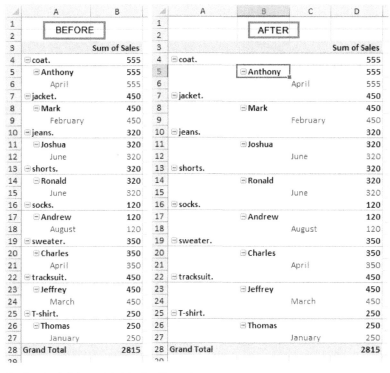

Refresh A Pivot Table In Excel

Although a pivot table report is linked to your source data, you may be shocked to learn that it is not automatically refreshed by Excel.

Any data changes may be obtained by manually initiating a refresh operation or by having it refresh automatically when you access the spreadsheet.

Manual Method

Click in the table wherever you want

On the *PivotTable Analyze* tab (*Data* group), click the *Refresh* command.

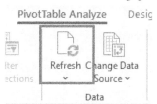

You may also right-click the table and choose Refresh from the context menu.

Automatic Method

This is works automatically when you open your workbook. To do this, follow the steps:

Click Options > Options in the PivotTable group on the PivotTable Analyze tab

Navigate to the *Data* tab in the *PivotTable Options* dialog box and click the *Refresh data upon opening the file* check box.

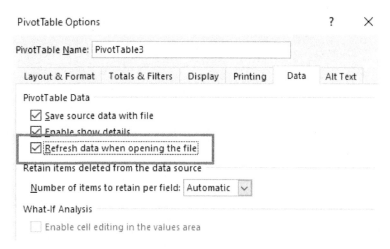

Move the Pivot Table

If you wish to relocate your table to a different workbook, worksheet, or another place in the current sheet, go to the *PivotTable Analyze* tab and choose the *Move PivotTable* button from the Actions group. Click OK after selecting a new destination.

Delete a Pivot Table

You may remove a summary report in a variety of ways if you no longer need it.

If your table is in a different worksheet, remove it. If your table is on a sheet with other data, select the whole pivot table with the mouse and hit the Delete key. To remove a pivot table, go to the *PivotTable Analyze* tab > *Actions* group, click the *Select* button, select *Entire PivotTable*, and then hit Delete.

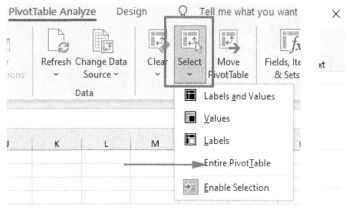

CHAPTER 15: NAMED RANGE

Introducing Named Range

What does 'Name' Mean in Excel?

People, artifacts, and geographical positions are commonly referred to by their names in daily life. Naturally, we say "New York City" instead of "the city located at latitude 40.7128°N and longitude 74.0059°W."

Similarly, in Excel, you can assign each cell, or any range of the cells, a user-friendly name and refer to cells by name instead of references.

Which one of the two formulas in the example is easier to understand?

You can build and use two types of names in Microsoft Excel:

- A term that corresponds to a single cell, several cells, a constant meaning, or formula is known as a defined name. A named set, or specified range, is created when you give a group of cells a name. These names are the topic of this chapter.

- When you place a table inside a worksheet (CTRL+T), an Excel table of that name is generated automatically. See How to Create and Use Tables in Excel for more details on Excel tables.

Creating A Named Range

Creating a Named Range

In Excel, there are three methods for defining a term: the Name Box, the Define Name key, and the Name Manager.

Type the name in a Name Box

The Name Box in Excel is the quickest way to name a range:

Choose any cell or group of cells that you'd like to name.

In the *Name Box*, type any name.

Enter the code by entering the key

Voilà, a newly named set of cells has been created!

Items _list

Create any name with the Defined Name option.

This is another way to build a named set in Excel:

- Choose a cell or range of cells.

- Click the Define Name key in the Define Names category on the Formulas tab.

- Three steps should be taken using the New Name dialog box:

- Type a range name in the Name box.

- Set your name scope in the Scope drop-down (this creates a default for the Workbook).

- Check that the term in the cell refers to the box and, if not, make the necessary changes.

- Click OK.

Note: Excel produces a name with full references by default. Delete the $ symbol from the reference if you want a related named range.

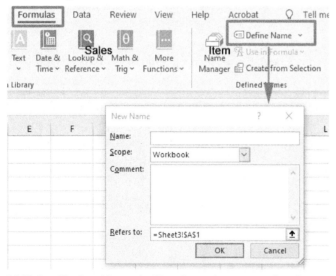

Utilizing Define Name in Excel requires a couple of extra clicks than the previous method. Nevertheless, it offers more options, including setting the scope of the name and giving the name a description. You can also use the Excel Define Name function to name formula or constant.

Create a named range with Name Manager in Excel

In Excel, the Name Manager function is typically used to deal with pre-existing names. It will, however, assist you in creating a new name. Here's how to do it: Tap Name Manager in the Formulas tab / Defined Name group. Alternatively, simply click CTRL+F3 (this is the preferred way).

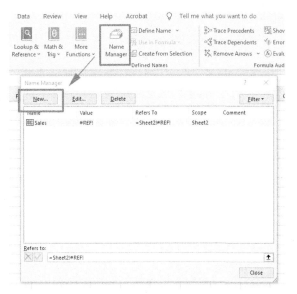

This will reveal a New Name dialog box, in which you can type the name as seen in the above section.

Select the newly produced name from the Name Box drop-down list to easily verify it. This setting is applied to a worksheet as soon as you release your mouse.

Creating a Name for a Constant in Excel

In comparison to named ranges, Excel enables you to create a named constant by defining a name with no cell reference. Use either the Define Name or Name Manager functions, as described above, to generate a name.

For example, you might want to use the name USD EUR (USD-EUR exchange rate) and a fixed number. In the 'Refers to' section, type the value followed by an equal sign (=), for example, =0.93:

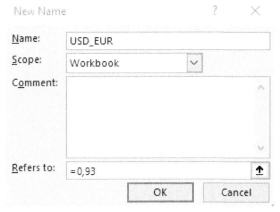

You can also utilize this name elsewhere in your USD-EUR conversion formulas:

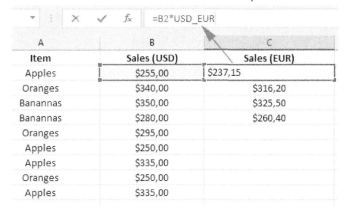

Item	Sales (USD)	Sales (EUR)
Apples	$255,00	$237,15
Oranges	$340,00	$316,20
Banannas	$350,00	$325,50
Banannas	$280,00	$260,40
Oranges	$295,00	
Apples	$250,00	
Apples	$335,00	
Oranges	$250,00	
Apples	$335,00	

You can adjust the value in one place when the rate of exchange increases, and all the numbers are recalculated in one step.

Defining any Name for a Formula

You can name an Excel formula in a similar way, such as one that returns a count of non-empty cells in column A, except for the header row (- 1): Sheet5! =COUNTA (Sheet 5! $A: $A) -1

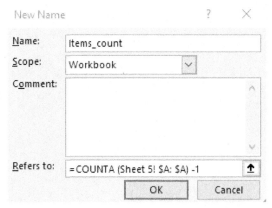

Now, in any cell, type an equal sign and the name of the formula to find out how many items are in column A on Sheet 5, except the column header: = Count of Items

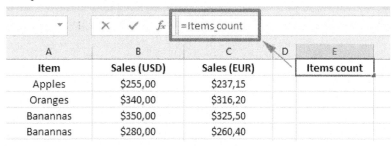

Item	Sales (USD)	Sales (EUR)		Items count
Apples	$255,00	$237,15		
Oranges	$340,00	$316,20		
Banannas	$350,00	$325,50		
Banannas	$280,00	$260,40		

Naming Columns in Excel

You can easily name a column and row if your data is organized in tabular format:

The whole table, including the column and row headers, should be selected.

Click the Create from Selection key in the Formula tab / Define Name group. Alternatively, use the CTRL+Shift+F3 keyboard shortcut.

The Create Names from the Selection dialog window will appear in either case. Press OK after selecting the header of either a row or a column, or both.

Since you have headers in the top row and left column in this case, choose these two options:

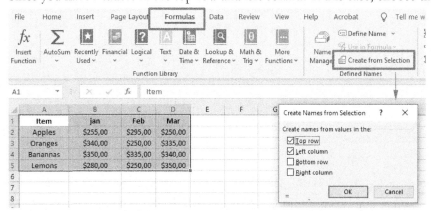

As a result, Excel builds seven named ranges according to the names in the headers:

Lemons, Apples, Bananas, and Oranges are arranged in rows.

The months of February, January, and March are mentioned in the columns.

⬚ Apples	{"$255","$295","$250"}	=Sheet3!$B$2:$D$2
⬚ Bananas	{"$350","$335","$340"}	=Sheet3!$B$4:$D$4
⬚ Feb	{"$295";"$250";"$33...	=Sheet3!$C$2:$C$5
⬚ Jan	{"$255";"$340";"$35...	=Sheet3!$B$2:$B$5
⬚ Lemons	{"$280","$250","$350"}	=Sheet3!$B$5:$D$5
⬚ Mar	{"$250";"$335";"$34...	=Sheet3!$D$2:$D$5
⬚ Oranges	{"$340","$250","$335"}	=Sheet3!$B$3:$D$3

The spaces in the header labels will be substituted with underscores (_) if there are any spaces between words.

Creating Dynamic Named Ranges In Excel

Excel Dynamic Named Range

You've been working with a static named range that often applies to similar cells in previous instances, which means you'll have to manually change the range selection anytime you want to introduce additional data to a named range.

When dealing with extensive data sets, it makes sense to build a complex named range that instantly accommodates additional data.

Excel allows you to create a dynamic range using the OFFSET formula.

Alternatively, to create a dynamic range, use the INDEX formula.

Rules When Creating Named Range

Naming Rules in Excel

There are some rules to remember while creating a name in Excel:

The length of the Excel name must be less than 255 characters.

Spaces and many punctuation characters cannot be used in Excel names.

A letter, backslash (\) or underscore (_), must be the first character in the name. Errors will occur if the name starts with something else.

When using names in Excel, the case is unimportant. "Apples," "apples," and "APPLES," for example, will all be viewed as an identical names.

Ranges cannot be named in the same way as cell references. That is, a range cannot be given the names "A1"/"AA1."

Besides the letters "r," "c," and "C," you could name any range with a single letter, such as "a,"/"b,"/"D," and so on (Such characters are utilized as shortcuts to select a column or row for a recently selected cell while you type these in the Name Box).

Benefits Of Creating Named Ranges In Excel

1. Excel names make formulas simpler to create and read

You might not have to write complicated references or go back and forth on your sheet selecting ranges.

Start entering a name you intend to use in a formula, and Excel can provide you with a collection of possible matches.

Double-click your desired name, and Excel can automatically insert it into the formula

2. Excel names allow you to create resilient formulas

You can construct a "dynamic" algorithm that automatically uses new details in equations without manually editing any corresponding data by utilizing dynamic labeled ranges.

3. Excel names make formulas simpler to re-use

It's a lot simpler to transfer formula to another sheet or transfer the formula to a new workbook when you use Excel names.

Generate the same name in the destination workbook and copy/paste your formula: you'll be up and running in no time.

Tip: Rather than copying a formula cell, copy the formula as text in the formula bar to prevent Excel from generating new names for this formula.

4. Named ranges to make navigation easier

Click on the name of a designated range in the Name box to access it easily. If a designated range is located on another document, Excel can immediately navigate to this sheet.

Note that, in Excel, complex named ranges don't appear in the Name box. Open the Excel Name Manager (CTRL+F3) to see the dynamic ranges. It displays the full information of all the names in the workbook, plus their scope and references.

5. Named ranges to allow dynamic drop-down lists to be created

Create a complex named range first; the data validation lists then depend on that to create an expandable and updatable drop-down list. You can find specific step-by-step guidelines here: How can you make a complex drop-down menu in Excel?

Useful Named Range Shortcuts (F3)

Excel Names Shortcuts

The most commonly used Excel tools can be accessed in a variety of ways, including the ribbon, the right-click menu, and keyboard shortcuts. Named ranges in Excel are no different. Here are three Excel shortcuts for working with names:

To access the Excel Name Manager, press CTRL+F3.

To build a named range from a set, press CTRL+Shift+F3.

Press F3 to see lists of all the names in the workbook.

Excel Name Error (#REF and #NAME)

Once you insert and remove cells in an established named set, Microsoft Excel does its best to keep the specified names consistent and accurate by automatically changing the range references. If you build the named range from cells A1: A10 and then insert a new row somewhere between rows 1 and 10, this same range reference becomes A1: A11. Similarly, deleting every cell from A1 to A10 would cause the named range to shrink.

If you remove any of the cells in a named range, the name becomes invalid, and the Name Manager shows a #REF! Error. In a formula with a reference of that name, a similar error will appear: A #NAME?

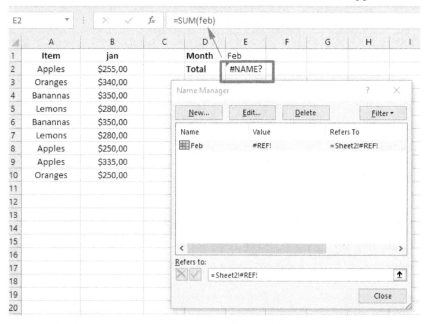

An error appears when a formula applies to a name that does not occur (due to a typo or deletion). In any event, open Excel Name Manager and double-check the names you've identified are still correct (this is the fastest method for filtering names with errors).

In Excel, that's how you make and use names.

For example, we may have a list of contacts we would like to use in formulas. We could either use A1:G17 to identify the range of data or name the range "Contacts" and then use that name to reference the data from then on.

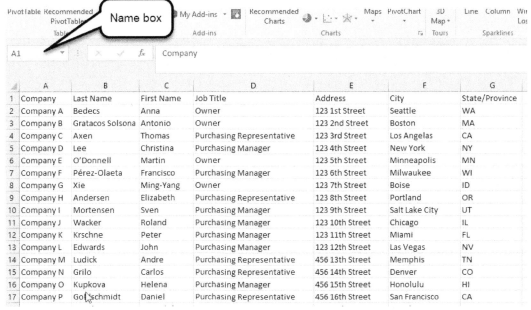

	A	B	C	D	E	F	G
1	Company	Last Name	First Name	Job Title	Address	City	State/Province
2	Company A	Bedecs	Anna	Owner	123 1st Street	Seattle	WA
3	Company B	Gratacos Solsona	Antonio	Owner	123 2nd Street	Boston	MA
4	Company C	Axen	Thomas	Purchasing Representative	123 3rd Street	Los Angelas	CA
5	Company D	Lee	Christina	Purchasing Manager	123 4th Street	New York	NY
6	Company E	O'Donnell	Martin	Owner	123 5th Street	Minneapolis	MN
7	Company F	Pérez-Olaeta	Francisco	Purchasing Manager	123 6th Street	Milwaukee	WI
8	Company G	Xie	Ming-Yang	Owner	123 7th Street	Boise	ID
9	Company H	Andersen	Elizabeth	Purchasing Representative	123 8th Street	Portland	OR
10	Company I	Mortensen	Sven	Purchasing Manager	123 9th Street	Salt Lake City	UT
11	Company J	Wacker	Roland	Purchasing Manager	123 10th Street	Chicago	IL
12	Company K	Krschne	Peter	Purchasing Manager	123 11th Street	Miami	FL
13	Company L	Edwards	John	Purchasing Manager	123 12th Street	Las Vegas	NV
14	Company M	Ludick	Andre	Purchasing Representative	456 13th Street	Memphis	TN
15	Company N	Grilo	Carlos	Purchasing Representative	456 14th Street	Denver	CO
16	Company O	Kupkova	Helena	Purchasing Manager	456 15th Street	Honolulu	HI
17	Company P	Goldschmidt	Daniel	Purchasing Representative	456 16th Street	San Francisco	CA

One of the benefits of using a named range is that the name is an absolute reference. When you create a formula with that name, you can copy and paste the formula into any part of your workbook, including different worksheets in the workbook, and the name will always point to the same group of cells.

How To Edit Named Ranges In Excel

Editing a Named Range

- On the Formulas tab, click Name Manager (in the Defined Names group).
- On the list, select the named range you want to edit and click on the Edit… button.

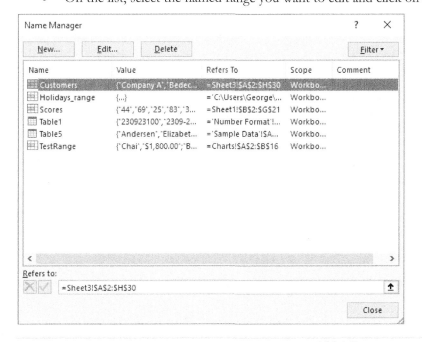

- Click OK on the Edit Name box.

- Click Close.

- Deleting a Named Range

- On the Formulas tab, click Name Manager.

- Select the named range you want to delete from the list.

- Click the Delete button.

- Click Close when done.

How to Use a Named Range

To select a named range, click the dropdown arrow of the name box and select the name from the dropdown list.

This will display the worksheet with the range (if you're on a different worksheet) and select all the rows and columns in the range.

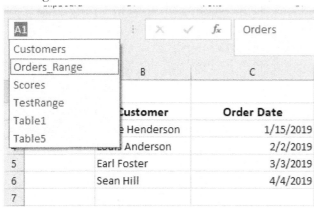

Example

The following example demonstrates the use of a named range called **Orders_Range** in place of the cell reference A1:D13. The example uses two formulas to count numeric values and blank cells in the range. The name of the range has been used as arguments in the functions instead of A1:D13.

=COUNT(Orders_Range)

=COUNTBLANK(Orders_Range)

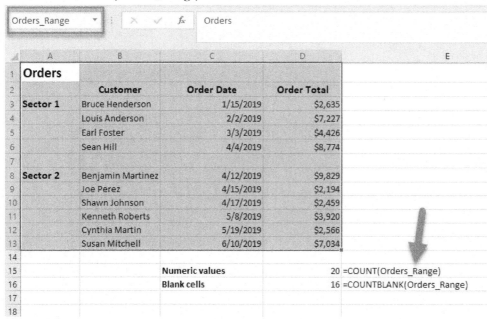

How You Can Filter Names in Excel

If a workbook has many titles, use the Filter key at the top right-hand corner of the Excel Name Manager window to see only those names that are currently appropriate. The following filters are available:

- Names that are exclusive to a worksheet or a workbook

- Names that contain or do not contain errors

- Table names or defined names

How You Can Delete Named Ranges in Excel

Find the named range in the Name Manager and press the Delete button to remove it.

To delete multiple names, select the first name, then press and hold the CTRL key when selecting the others you would like to remove. Press the Delete key to delete all the selected names at once.

How You Can Delete Defined Name with Errors

If you have many invalid names or defined names with errors, you can manage them using the Filter button / Names with Errors:

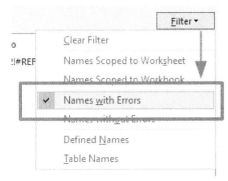

Then, as mentioned above (while holding down the Shift key), select all the filtered names and press the Delete key.

Note: If any Excel names had been included in the calculations, make sure to correct them before removing them, or your formulas will generate an error such as #NAME? Errors.

CHAPTER 16: VLOOKUP

What Does The Vlookup Function Do, And How Does It Work?

VLOOKUP is one of these functions. The main use of VLOOKUP is to match data with common information. For example, if one Excel file contains hundreds of zip codes but no cities, we can use VLOOKUP to match and populate the city names using another file with a list of both zip codes and cities.

The VLOOKUP Function is an extremely powerful and versatile way to use Excel. You can use it to find a matching data point from another table and then perform mathematical calculations with the results. You can also mash results together in many other ways.

So, how do we call the VLOOKUP function? As for all functions in Excel, we start with an equal sign (=) in a cell.

WAIT! You might be accustomed to using a Function Arguments box like this one.

While I cannot stop you from using the Function Arguments box, the purpose of this book is to sharpen your Excel skills and prepare you for work in a professional setting. If you use VLOOKUP on occasion, using the arguments box is acceptable. If you use VLOOKUP and other functions frequently, your productivity will suffer using this method.

I recommend typing the information into the cell so you can see the syntax you are using. You might ask, "What if I make a mistake?" Of course, you will! Making mistakes is extremely valuable, and the arguments box does not allow you to make egregious errors.

When you rode your bike with training wheels, bowled with bumpers, or wore a napkin like a bib, there was a point when you decided to stop. Please make that conscious decision now with regard to VLOOKUP's Function Arguments box.

Formulas and functions are ways we communicate with Excel to get the answers we are seeking. Often functions require *arguments* or *parameters*. These are pieces of information that Excel requires to understand exactly what we are looking for.

The Structure of a VLOOKUP

When writing a VLOOKUP function, always keep in mind:

- *The needle* – What am I seeking?

- *The haystack* – Where am I looking for it?

- *The column index* – What is the distance from my "needle" to the column with the answer?

- *The range lookup* – Am I using a range of values or not?

I created the preceding diagram to provide some additional visual context. These four parameters are the nuts and bolts of the VLOOKUP function. I will provide a brief overview describing these components; then, we will dive into the details of each in the chapters that follow.

Lookup Value

The first parameter we provide is the *lookup value* – our needle. The lookup value is the identifying information for the row we are trying to match.

Picture a grade school attendance booklet with student names down the left side and dates across the top. Each day, missing students have marked absent with a capital A in that date's column and their individual rows. If we are looking at the booklet and want to see if Billy was absent last week, we would start by looking for the row with Billy's name in it. In this case, *Billy* is the lookup value.

Table Array

The second parameter is the table array, illustrated earlier as a haystack. This defines the search area. The table array consists of beginning and end points – two cell addresses separated by a colon (:), where the first address identifies the top-left cell and the second address marks the cell at the bottom right. If we enter M45:P50 as the parameter for the table array, then Excel will look at the following cells in our VLOOKUP function:

M45 N45 O45 P45	M47 N47 O47 P47	M49 N49 O49 P49
M46 N46 O46 P46	M48 N48 O48 P48	M50 N50 O50 P50

Column Index

The third parameter is the column index. It is the number of columns to count, beginning from the left side of the search area. It tells Excel that once my lookup value is found in the leftmost column, move that many cells to the right – on that specific row – to find the answer.

If the lookup value describes which floor to press on an elevator, and the table array describes which building we need to be in, the column index tells us what number is on the door.

Range

The fourth parameter is the range, and it tells Excel whether we are using VLOOKUP to determine if our value is either within a specified range of values or an exact match. At this point, we will use 0 or FALSE for this argument to seek out an exact match. Later in the book, we will cover the details related to a VLOOKUP range argument with a 1 or TRUE value, although its use is limited.

With any function in the formula bar, if you point anywhere inside the parentheses, you will notice the parameters of the function displayed beneath it. To identify a parameter as optional, Excel puts brackets ([ ]) around it.

f_x	=VLOOKUP(A2,B1:D25,2,0|
C	VLOOKUP(lookup_value, table_array, col_index_num, **[range_lookup]**)

As you just learned, VLOOKUP requires a lookup value to search for, a table array to reference, the column index within that table, and a range. Notice that the last parameter in the preceding illustration ([range_lookup]), which Excel is telling us, is optional, but it is not. In this case, don't believe it. You will see why when we look more closely at the range parameter.

Basic Knowledge

When working with VLOOKUP functions, it is important to know and remember the next four points. They will help maintain your sanity and possibly assist your troubleshooting if the value returned is unexpected:

VLOOKUP only searches from left to right. There is no option to search from right to left. Excel will only find the lookup value if it exists in the leftmost column of the table array. If you have the lookup value in a column to the right of the value you want to return, you will need to copy the lookup value's column to the right of your table or use other methods discussed later.

Looking at the following illustration, this means if the Status column has the information you want to be returned and the Book column contains your lookup value, then to access the information in the Status column with VLOOKUP, you must copy it into or after the column C, so the Book column is first in the table array.

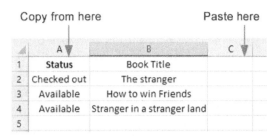

As you can see above, by copying and pasting the status column the lookup value column (Book) will come first

VLOOKUP is lazy. It always returns the first match in the table. If there are three or four occurrences of the lookup value in the column, only the first row with matching information will be returned.

That means if a class list has two students named Charles, using VLOOKUP to find the second student on the list will not work. Again, based on your needs, there are methods to work around this, such as searching for the students' full names by joining (or *concatenating*) the first and last names. For more on this method, see the "Concatenate VLOOKUP" section.

VLOOKUP is not case-sensitive. If you look for "POND SCUM" and "pond scum" (or "Pond Scum") is on the list, VLOOKUP will return that row.

VLOOKUP's fourth parameter, range lookup, can be misleading. Most matches you look for will be exact matches, which requires you to use 0 or FALSE for this parameter. Omitting the range argument will imply that its value is TRUE and open up the possibility of problems. Does it matter whether you use 0 or FALSE? No, it is simply a matter of preference.

MAIN CAUSES OF ERRORS WITH VLOOKUP

An error in Excel is a text that warns you that something in your formula or argument is incorrect. Excel tells you the type of Error you are facing so you know how to solve it.

In VLOOKUP you can usually find 4 types of Errors: #N/A, #REF!, #Value! And #Name!.

#N/A ERROR

What does this one warn?

This error indicates that your formula didn't find the Lookup Value in the Table Array.

When does it happen?

When the Lookup Value doesn't exist in the first column of the Table Array. It may be because the Table Array points to a range outside the database.

It also occurs when the Lookup Value is slightly different in the database. For example, "id12" without intermediate space is not the same as "id 12" with intermediate space.

The error of "Sylvia Bramee" happens because the database is written in a different way than "Sylvia Brame." For that reason, Vlookup doesn't "find" it.

The error of Jonh Smith occurs because it doesn't even exist in the database; obviously, Vlookup doesn't find it.

The error of Delilah Ridge and Markita Pryzbyla is due to the lack of absolute references; both names are outside the Table Array; therefore, Vlookup does not find them and returns #N/A.

How to fix it?

Step 1: Confirm that the Lookup value doesn't have spaces at the beginning, middle or end. Remember that for Vlookup to work the Lookup Value must match and be written just like in the database.

Step 2: Check that the Table Array you chose is correctly positioned in each formula you wrote. Forgetting to use absolute references is the main cause of #N/A.

Remember:

Forgetting to use the Absolute References in the Table Array is the main cause of #N/A

#REF! ERROR

What does this one warn?

#REF! error tells you that within your formula, you refer to a cell that is not valid for that formula.

When does it happen?

It happens when you have a written formula, for example, =VLOOKUP(A3,$F$2:$G$9,2,0), and then you delete a cell that you included in the formula. Suppose you delete column A by having A3 in the first argument of the formula. In this

case, the result will show #REF! and if you want to read the formula, the error will appear
like this =VLOOKUP(#REF!,$F$2:$G$9,2,0)

Another reason why #REF! occurs is because a column number that does not exist (within the Table Array) is written in the 3rd argument. For example: If you have $F$2:$G$9 as Table Array (2 columns), the maximum number in Column Index Number should be 2. With a Table Array of 2 columns and a Column Index Number of 3, you will get a #REF!

Now "Sylvia Brame" is well written, no longer shows #N/A but shows #REF! What's going on?

If we look at the formula, we can see that the third argument (Column Index Number) is 5 when the Table Array only contains 4 columns that are D, E, F, and G (Column G does not appear in the image because it contains the annual sales that are irrelevant to this example).

Then because column 5 of the Table Array doesn't exist, Excel shows #REF!. The solution is to change the 5 to a 3.

How to solve it?

Step 1: If you deleted any column, row, or cell. Modify the formula manually. This is the most common cause. When you shape your spreadsheet, it is common to delete cells, causing the #REF error!

Step 2: Verify that the Column Index Number doesn't exceed the number of columns that the Table Array has.

#VALUE! ERROR

What does this one warn?

Indicates that your formula is wrong, and normally the problem is found in the third argument, column index number.

When does it happen?

This error is more common in nested formulas (formulas that contain other formulas within them). In nested formulas, it is likely that the value in Column Index Number is 0 or negative. In this case, #VALUE appears.

The same example with Sylvia Brame, now she has the error #VALUE! (#VALOR! In Spanish). What's going on?

In the third argument, the Column Index Number is a 0 instead of a column number.

How to solve it?

Step 1: Directly look at the third argument. Check that it doesn't contain any number of columns greater than the Table Array, no negative number or 0.

#NAME! ERROR

What does this one warn?

The name of your formula is misspelled, or an argument that requires a number has text.

When does it happen?

If you write a wrong formula name, this error appears. For example, if instead of =VLOOKUP you write =VLOOKUO or =VLOOLUP the result will be the #NAME error.

If in the Column Index Number argument you type Text instead of Numbers, you also get the error.

The Range Lookup argument only supports 4 options: TRUE, FALSE, 1 and 0. If you write anything else in that argument, you will get the #NAME! Error too.

Now you have 3 #NAME! errors (#NOMBRE! In Spanish). What's going on? The formulas must be revised one by one to discover what happens.

Tesha Mooney's formula is misspelled, indicating "VLOOKU" instead of "VLOOKUP". That causes the #NAME! error.

Sook's formula has a letter in the Column Index Number argument; that argument only accepts numbers. That causes the #NAME!

Markita's formula has a letter within the fourth argument that only accepts 0, 1, TRUE or FALSE. That causes the #NAME!.

How to solve it?

Step 1: Check that your formula is well written.

Step 2: Check the Column Index Number argument, it should only contain numbers.

Step 3: Check the Range Lookup argument, you only have 4 options in that argument.

How To Use A Vlookup Pulling Data From Another Spreadsheet (Controlla Bene)

As we alredy discuss, you can access each worksheet at the bottom of the spreadsheet, you will find them as small tabs.

Benefits of Using Vlookup Trough Different Worksheets

You already know that Vlookup can get information from a database (that you specify in your argument Array Table) to make the job easier and faster. But *most of the time, the databases are in another worksheet.*

With VLOOKUP you can bring information from a different worksheet without any problem. One of the advantages of having your database in another worksheet is that you have less visible information, and your work looks cleaner and more professional.

How Is Vlookup Used Through Worksheets?

The simplest form of lookup value is the *literal lookup value.* This means you enter the exact value for which you are looking.

When entering a literal value as a lookup value, it is just that – literally entering what we are seeking. Now, I will literally show you what I mean in the following example.

Let's have a look at the following example. People are sitting in seats represented by cells and in rows represented by, well, rows. Column A contains the name of the person sitting in the aisle seat at the beginning of the row. Coincidentally, each of their names is a palindrome, the point of which escapes me.

	A	B
1	Beginning of Row	Next Seat
2	Otto	Jordan
3	Sylys	George
4	Hannah	Peter
5	Anna	Victor
6	Ava	Jen
7	Elle	Larry
8	Bob	Yvette
9	Eve	Josephine
10	JJ	Eleanor

Consider typing this formula into cell E5:

=VLOOKUP("Hannah",A1:B10,2,0)

The characters *Hannah* are the literal reference we are looking up. If I was returning from the restroom and the usher asked where I was sitting, and I yelled, "Hey, Hannah!" then I would be looking for my seat using a similar method. It is effective, although not the way a professional usher would expect you to find your seat.

When referring to a *literal reference*, we are spelling out the lookup value within the VLOOKUP formula by putting a term in quotation marks and placing it into the formula, like "Hannah."

If we type this formula in cell E3:

=VLOOKUP("Eve",A1:B10,2,0)

The result will be Josephine. The lookup value here is *Eve,* and, once again, it is a literal reference. Therefore, literal references are taking the actual reference.

What lookup value would you use to see George as a result? Try one or two more, and then we will look at another example of a literal lookup value.

An important note is that your lookup value always comes from the first column of the table array. If we wanted to use *Yvette* from column B as my lookup value, we would need to change the table array accordingly, as shown earlier. With the Palindromes worksheet's current arrangement, there is no VLOOKUP method we can use to return Bob by using *Yvette.*

Literally No Quotes

You may believe the rule is to place all literal references in quotation marks, but you would believe something untrue, you will stand corrected. There are times we use quotation marks, and there are times we do not.

For character (a single letter or a number to be treated as text) or any *string* (a geek word for a cluster of characters), we surround our lookup value with quotation marks (" "). When searching using a numeric value, we do not use quotation marks.

Now, go to the worksheet named Photographic Memory in the companion file.

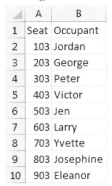

	A	B
1	Seat	Occupant
2	103	Jordan
3	203	George
4	303	Peter
5	403	Victor
6	503	Jen
7	603	Larry
8	703	Yvette
9	803	Josephine
10	903	Eleanor

If I possessed a photographic memory, was at the stadium with my hands full of goodies from the refreshment stand, and recalled my seat number from memory, I would tell the usher, "I am in seat 303." The VLOOKUP for that would look like this:

=VLOOKUP(303,A1:B10,2,0)

This is because numeric values do not require quotation marks. If we use quotations marks and type:

=VLOOKUP("303",A1:B10,2,0)

Excel will return an error indicating the value cannot be found. When we use quotation marks, Excel thinks we are speaking in text, not numbers. Make sure whichever is in the lookup value – a numeric value or a number treated as text – matches the cell contents you are referencing. At this point, we know we can use VLOOKUP with a literal lookup value, and this value can be text or numeric. We also know several names that are palindromes, and some of my friends with these names spell them backward.

Referenced Value

If you said you were unimpressed with literal references, I would agree. By itself, a literal reference has little practical use, and I do not see how my life will be stress-free or enlightened when utilizing literal references in VLOOKUP. But what if I use a lookup value to demonstrate something more profound? What if I introduce a method to avoid typing every lookup value into a cell? I will show you what I just described now.

Bring in the referenced value.

A referenced value uses a reference to a cell – instead of a literal value – as the lookup value. Essentially, we're pointing to a cell and declaring, "I want to find a cell matching the contents of this cell," instead of typing it in.

We will return to the Palindromes worksheet to illustrate this.

Follow these instructions to set up the worksheet.

- Select cell A4 and copy its contents.

- Select cell D5 and paste it into that cell. Hannah should now appear in cell D5.

- Now type the following into cell E5:

=VLOOKUP(D5,A1:B10,2,0)

	A	B	C	D	E
1	Beginning of Row	Next Seat			
2	Otto	Jordan			
3	Sylys	George			
4	Hannah	Peter			
5	Anna	Victor		Hannah	Peter
6	Ava	Jen			
7	Elle	Larry			
8	Bob	Yvette			
9	Eve	Josephine			
10	JJ	Eleanor			

By using D5 as the first argument of the VLOOKUP, you told Excel to use the contents of cell D5 as the lookup value rather than the literal value *Hannah*. You pointed to Hannah by using D5 rather than typing out the name. This is a more standard method for using VLOOKUP.

What is the difference?

Type *Elle* into cell D5. As we see in the following illustration, Peter is replaced by Larry in cell E5. This happens because cell D5 now contains Elle, not Hannah. The formula is neutral to whatever value is in the referenced cell, and the contents of D5 dictate the value in E5. If we changed D5 to *Anna*, then the value in E5 would change to Victor.

	A	B	C	D	E
1	Beginning of Row	Next Seat			
2	Otto	Jordan			
3	Sylys	George			
4	Hannah	Peter			
5	Anna	Victor		Elle	Larry
6	Ava	Jen			
7	Elle	Larry			
8	Bob	Yvette			
9	Eve	Josephine			
10	JJ	Eleanor			

Now, type the name *Otto* into cell D9 to demonstrate another point.

Referenced lookup values provide a lot of flexibility in terms of pulling data together from multiple sources. Note that we do not need to keep our referenced value adjacent to our VLOOKUP formula. We can call our reference from anywhere to obtain a value.

If we type the following in cell Z35, we will still get a result:

=VLOOKUP(D9,A1:B10,2,0)

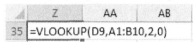

	Z	AA	AB
35	=VLOOKUP(D9,A1:B10,2,0)		

Can you guess the value?

We are referencing cell D9, so we will get the name next to Otto. The name next to Otto in cell A2 is Jordan, and Jordan is the value returned.

We can place D9 – the needle – anywhere. In this case, the needle is a cell pointing to Otto. Cells A1 through B10 are the table array – or haystack – and the column index (2) instructs Excel to look at two columns to the right starting from and including column A. This is why the result is Jordan.

Try this in any empty cells within the Palindromes worksheet to see if you can replicate this. For example, how can you get the name Jordan as a result in cell BE389?

Now replace the name Otto with =*A2*. Look back at cell Z35, and you'll see that Jordan shows as the value. We can see from here that a reference to a reference is also valid as a lookup value.

How To Write A Simple Vlookup Formula?

Syntax and Arguments
The range_lookup is FALSE, which tells VLOOKUP that we want an exact match.

To look up the Reorder Level for Dried Pears we use the same formula and just change the col_index_num argument to 3, meaning we want to return values from the third column in table_array, which is the Reorder Level column.

=VLOOKUP(G2, B2:D46, 3, FALSE)

Here, the VLOOKUP search for Dried Pears returns a Reorder Level of 10.

Finding an Approximate Match with VLOOKUP

We want to ensure that if an exact match is not found on the commission table that an approximate match is applied for the sales rep. $5,000 or more in sales is 2% commission, $10,000 or more is 5%, $20,000 or more is 10%, and so on.

Formula Explanation

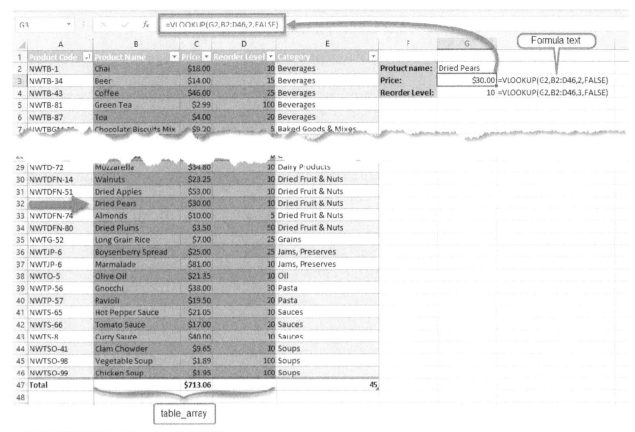

=VLOOKUP(B3,table_array,2,TRUE)

The lookup_value is cell B3 which is the value for which we want an approximate match in the lookup range (cells E3:F9).

Note that the lookup range (E3:F9) is named table_array. This is known as a named range. The benefit of using named ranges in formulas you want to fill down is that a named range is an absolute reference. This ensures the cell references you want to remain the same will not change as you fill down the formula.

Using VLOOKUP and the CHOOSE Function for Left Lookups

In this example, we want to add the product code to the list of orders on the left of the worksheet below. The product codes can be found in the Product list to the right of the Orders.

One limitation of VLOOKUP is that we can only return values in a column to the right of the lookup range.

To solve this problem, we can use the CHOOSE function to rearrange the columns for the table_array argument of VLOOKUP.

A Quick Look at the CHOOSE Function Before progressing to the example, we need to first look at what the CHOOSE function does.

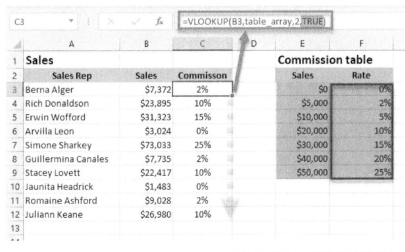

MODULE F

CHAPTER 17: TIPS AND TRICKS

Customize The Dates

The Customized cell format allows you to change the layout of a period in a cell. To do so, type a date in such a cell, select Format, Cells, Standard in the Category, window, Type, input box, and M repeatedly until the correct format appears in the Sample field.

Column Copy Quickly

By clicking doubled on a cell's handle, you might fill out cells in such a column. Excel can duplicate the tapped cell in any of the cells below it, stopping until it approaches a cell without blanks on both sides.

Merge Cell Contents

Click on cell C1 and type =A1&B1 to combine the data of cells B1 and A1. Since the product is a text string rather than a sum, combining 10 and 7 yields 107 rather than 17.

	A	B	C
1	10	7	107
2			

Dynamic Formatting

Excel may be configured to warn you of important figures in the cell by changing the text's size and color when a certain requirement is met. Select a cell (for example, the cell containing your bank balance total) and choose Type, Conditional formatting... In the pop-up dialogue, choose the conditions (E.g., "Cell value < 0") and press the Format... icon. Now, in the Color list box, choose a new color and press OK. To end, click OK once more. Whenever your chosen figure goes below zero, Excel can now represent it in the new color.

Cell's Border Connector

By selecting a group of similar cells and clicking Format Cells, choosing the Border section, and clicking the Outline icon, you may create a border around them – for example, all the totals.

Cellsentries Should Be Reduced In Size To Fit Their Cells

Using Shrink to Suit choice in Excel, you will compel Spreadsheets to access the entire text. Select Format, Cells>>Alignment tab >> check the Shrink to Matchbox. The more texts you get, the smaller the cell would be, but this isn't realistic for tiny cells with a ton of material.

Create Hyperlinks

Enter a name for the connection in a cell and press CTRL + K to position connections in cells that allow you to launch other documents with a single click. Select File... from the drop-down menu. Go to the file you want to connect to and choose it. Double-click it and then choose OK. Excel can now switch to the file anytime you select in that cell.

Convert Rows To Columns

By selecting the cells, you would like to turn around, going to Edit, Copy, choosing a new cell, and then moving to Edit, Paste Special, you can transform columns into a row and vice versa. Finally, press OK after ticking the Transpose button on the dialogue box.

Calculate Time

Put the formula =A2-A1 in a cell, where the earlier date and A2 are later. Remember to convert the reference cell to numeric form by highlighting it, going to Format, Cells..., choosing the Number column, and clicking Number from the Category list.

Enter "Url" As Text

Add an apostrophe at the URL start, such as www.futureplan.com, to discourage Excel from turning written Web sites into hyperlinks.

Calculate Cumulative Sum

Column A should contain the number to be inserted, such as A1 to A5, and column B should contain the formula =SUM ($A$1: A1). Go to Edit, Filled, Down, and choose the cells beside ones with a number (in our case, B1 to B5). The cumulative sum of the numbers in columns A1 through A5 is placed in the adjacent section.

Remove Hyperlinks

Suppose Excel already has converted the written URL to a hyperlink. In that case, you will undo it just by right-clicking on the offensive address and clicking Hyperlink. Delete Hyperlink from the pop-up menu.

Set Decimal Points

Click the Edit tab from the Tools, Choice, and Edit tab menus. To fix the numbers of decimal points, position a click in the Set decimal checkbox and then use the arrow in the Places.

Sort The Columns Quickly

Selecting a column and clicking the Sort Increasing or Sort Decreasing buttons is the easiest way to sort it into a hierarchy

Typing While Erasing Entries

If you type the formula incorrectly, click Esc to clear the contents of the cell.

Enter A Sequence Of Number

Press the CTRL key when typing the very first number inside a cell, then click, keep, and drag the cell's handle until you've hit the appropriate number of cells. First, release the mouse button, then the CTRL key.

Fit Tables To The Page

Click File, Page Configuration, select the Page section, click the Match to radio icon, and choose 1 page wide to allow the tables to fit on the page exactly. Click Delete on the tall box, which will now be clean.

Hide The Data

Highlight the appropriate cell and choose Format, Cells... to mask some confidential data from view. To render the data available again, go to the Numbers tab, pick Custom from Category: Chart, click doubled on the Type, input box, and enter, then undo the procedure.

Lotus Users' Assistant

If you've switched from Lotus 1 to 2 to 3 and are having trouble with Excel, you can get assistance tailored to your circumstance by supporting Lotus 1 to 2 to 3 Help.

Formula Browser

Select a cell and use "Paste" on the main toolbar to paste the formula. Select the required feature from the list box. Now press OK after clicking the cells in which one you like the target to execute the action.

Currently Active Cell

If you miss your location when browsing through your spreadsheet, click the CTRL Backspace keys to return to the actual active cell.

See The Bigger Image

You might like to move to Full display mode if you're operating on a big sheet: clicking on View, Full Display. To switch to a regular browser, click it again.

Automatically Fit The Text

Find the correct column and click Format>>column>>AutoFit Selection to make your job appear neater.

Fast Copy

It's fast to repeat the equation or figure inside the cells above the one you're in by pressing CTRL + '.

Easy And Fast Multiple Entry

Choose the target cells, type the formula as normal, and click CTRL + Enter if you need to type a formula in multiple cells at once.

Auto Selection

By keeping down CTRL when clicking on the individual cells, you may pick unconnected cells.

Re-Coloring The Lines

By going to Tools, Options, View, selecting the Color, List box, and picking a new color from the palette, you can adjust the color of the grid. Choosing white essentially eliminates the grid.

Angle Your Entry

Select the toolbar with the help of right-clicking, choose Chart, and choose one of the "ab" icons on the current toolbar to render Excel display text in the cell at a 45-degree angle. Change the text to whatever angle you like; if you want customized angles, click on the cells & choose Layout Cell from the pop-up screen, choose the Alignment tab, click on the Text marker in the Orientation pane, and move the Text pointer.

Zoom In

By highlighting the appropriate cells, selecting the arrows on the Zoom button on the toolbar, and choosing Selection from the chart, you can make Excel show just the field you're working in.

Another Standard Entry Path

When you click [Return] while editing cells, the mouse goes away. Click Tools, Options..., and then Edit to adjust the course. After entering the list box, click the Move selection button and choose another course from the drop-down menu.

See Formulas

By going to Tools, Options..., choose the Display tab, and ticking the Formulas check button, you can see all of the formulas at once.

Highlight Cells

Using the Special functions, you may pick all cells of a certain kind. Click Edit, Go To..., then Special..., choose the cell form from the dialogue box, and click OK.

Switch Off 0s

By choosing Tools, Options..., the Display tab, or unticking the 0-values tick box, you will prevent 0s from filling up your sheets.

How To Reference Worksheets In Another Workbook

You can reference worksheets in other worksheets within the same workbook, enter the name of the worksheet in addition to an exclamation sign (!). This mark should come before the cell address.

Therefore, if you want to refer to cell A1 in Sheet 2, you should enter Sheet 2!

How to Reference other Worksheets

Here are ways to reference another worksheet in Excel:

1. Tap on the cell where you want to type in the formula.

2. Enter the equal sign (=), including the formula you want to use.

3. To reference the worksheet, press the tab.

4. Choose the cell or group of cells you want to reference.

Using the Relative References

You can use relative references to create and copy a formula. Simply choose the cell containing the formula. To estimate the proper value, enter the formula. Then, go to your keyboard and press Enter.

Scroll to the fill handle at the lower right side of the chosen cell. Press down and drag the fill handle over the cells you want to fill.

Using the Absolute Reference in Creating and Duplicating a Formula

To create and edit a formula using absolute references, copy the formula you entered with absolute references. This will enable you to preserve the cell references. Then, choose the cell with the formula and copy it using CTRL + C.

Now, you can tap the destination cell where you decide to paste the formula. However, the cell references will definitely change. When you copy a formula 2 rows to the right, the cell references in the formula will shift 2 cells to the right side.

CHAPTER 18: COMMON ERRORS

Printing Difficulties

Excel 2010 to 2016: This is also a bug that is often found. When a user tries to print from a specific region inside a spreadsheet, it generates a page break for each and every cell, including the user's best efforts to fit the collection into one page. And it gives a margin error any time a user tries to scale the image.

Well, this is a really inconvenient problem, so learn about the most popular causes and how to fix the Excel printing mistake.

Causes include:

- It has been discovered that the problem arises as a result of the following circumstances:
- The printer driver has been corrupted.
- Alternatively, the customer does not have a default printer driver installed.

Resolution:

To resolve the problem, it is suggested that the printer driver be updated and that a new printer driver be used as the default printer driver. To do so, obey these instructions:

- To begin, open the Add Printer dialogue box as follows:
- Select Add a printer from the drop-down menu.
- Select Add a local printer from the Add Printer box.
- And then select Use an existing port, then Next.
- Now, select Microsoft from the Manufacturer drop-down menu.
- Next, select Microsoft XPS Document Writer.
- After that, select Use the currently configured driver (recommended) > Next.
- Pick Set as the default printer from the drop-down menu, then clicks Next.
- Finally, press the Finish button.

Verify that changing printer drivers resolves the problem:

- Excel can be used to open the spreadsheet.
- Select *File* > Print from the drop-down menu, then press the Print button.
- Found Unreadable Content

This is a typical Excel error that users encounter when they try to open an XlsxWriter file and receive the following message:

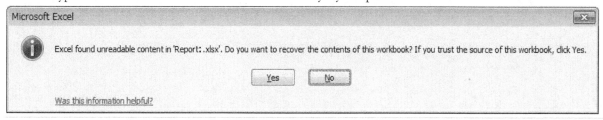

This challenging error in Excel's default alert about any validation error in XML used for the elements of the XLSX file, it is realized that the text is unreadable error is caused by the corruption of the whole Excel file or the corruption of one or more objects in the Excel file.

However, there are several manual methods that may assist in the correction of Excel errors. To obey all of the corrections,

Added formulas Performance Problems:

Excel users have complained about the slow performance. In XLSX Excel formats, formulas with a connection to an entire column may cause performance issues. In particular, formulas that reference an entire column in XLSX Excel formats can create performance issues.

This is due to the expanded column size of the most recent Excel..

Users must adjust the slow-calculating worksheets in Excel to make them compute tens, hundreds, or maybe even thousands of times quicker. To do so, switch the calculation modes from automated to manual. This will help you prevent the Excel output issues caused by added formulas.

Pasting Error

Excel pasting error is a very annoying error that consumers encounter from time to time when pasting details/data from one Excel document to another.

This mistake isn't exclusive to one Excel text, but it affects a number of them. "The details you are attempting to paste do not fit the cell type (Currency, Text, Date, or other formats) for the cells in the column," says the error message.

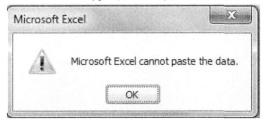

The primary cause of the mistake is yet to be determined. However, to correct the Excel error of being unable to paste results, use the following solution:

- If you're attempting to paste a vast volume of data, make sure the cell structure for the cells in the column fits the structure of the data you're pasting, and then paste the data one column at a time.

- You may also fix the error by changing the cell format for a column.

- To do so, follow these steps:

- First, press the column heading for the column that needs to be changed (A, B, C, and so on).

- Then, on the *Home* page, choose Number Format from the drop-down menu.

- After that, choose the cell format that corresponds to the data you're trying to paste into the column.

They hope that the provided solutions will assist you in resolving popular Excel errors; however, if the error persists despite following the provided solutions, please contact us. In this scenario, use the automatic Excel problem-solving approach to quickly get back to work on your Excel application.

Copy the Formula

To easily copy a formula, use the following steps:

- Hovering over a cell with the formula in the bottom-right corner (one will see that the pointer has become a thick black +)

- Press the black + sign twice.

- Taking formulas or Values and Pasting Them • If this technique doesn't fit because the range starts at a blank cell and ends at a blank cell, or one does not want to pull a formula down to Thousand rows, do this instead: • Select the first cell one want to copy or fill in with data.

- In the name box, write the address of the last cell in the range where one wants to enter the data or the formula, then press Shift + Enter.

- To modify the formula in the first cell, press F2.

- Finally, press CTRL + Enter.

IFERROR

When the formula produces a mistake, the Excel IFERROR feature returns a custom outcome, and when no error is found, it returns a normal result. IFERROR is a simple way to catch and handle errors without the need for nested IF statements.

Formula: =IFERROR (value, value if error)

Parameters:

Value is the value, or algorithm or reference, that would be used to look for errors.

Value if the error is the value of the outcome if a mistake is present.

When an error is found in a calculation, the IFERROR algorithm "catches" the error and returns an alternate answer or formula.

The IFERROR module may be used to catch and treat errors caused by other functions or formulas. The following errors are detected by IFERROR: #REF!, #DIV/0!, #VALUE!, #NUM!, #NULL! Or #NAME?

If A1 includes 10, B1 is empty, and C1 includes the formula =A1/B1, this IFERROR will catch the mistake #DIV/0 that is caused by dividing A1/B1

=IFERROR (A1/B1, please fill in the blanks in B1")

If B1 is null or void, C1 will show the message "Please insert a value in B1" as long as B1 is empty. The formula would return the product of A1/B1 when a number is inserted in B1.

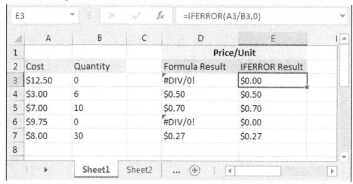

IFNA

When the formula produces a #N/A error, the IFNA function displays the customized result, and when no mistake is found, it returns a normal outcome.

IFNA is a clever way to capture and treat #N/A error when ignoring any other errors.

Formula: =IFNA (value, value_if_na)

Parameters:

Value is The value or algorithm, or reference that would be used to look for errors.

Value if na is if there is a #N/A mistake, this will be the value to be returned. The following is an illustration of IFNA being used to capture #N/A errors with VLOOKUP: =IFNA (VLOOKUP(A1,table,2,0),"Not found")

As a value is blank, it is treated as a blank string ("") rather than a mistake.

If value if na is set to a blank string (""), when a mistake occurs, no message is shown.

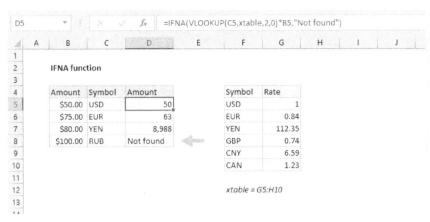

Formulas Not Working

It's possible that when one confirms a formula (by pressing enter), the answer doesn't appear; rather, The formula is shown in the cell.

| Number 1 | 40 |
| Number 2 | 50 |

Sum   =E6+E5 ← *The cell displays the formula & not the result*

The Solution is The issue is that the cell is formatted as text, so Excel interprets the formula as text.

Simply transform the cell to a Number/ General format, then verify the formula.

Formula View

This occurs more often by chance when the spreadsheet displays all calculations but not their output.

The entire spreadsheet is showing formulas & not the result

The Solution is to Simply click CTRL ~ again to return to regular mode.

Hashes in the Cell

Sometimes the cells would be loaded up with hashes. This may be because the cell data does not fit in the cell's width. The data is in excess of 253 letters A -ve number in the cell has been configured as a Date or Time format. Note the date or time must be positive numbers. The Fix is to Widen the column's width. For autofit, Shortcut is ALT OCA, or ALT OCW is for specific custom width) Reduce the no of characters in the cell value.

Please ensure the cell does not have a -ve number that is formatted as the date or time.

Page Breaks

Page breaks are innocuous, and they make the spreadsheet untidy.

The Solution is to Go to Options, then to Advanced, then to Scroll down to look for displaying options for the current spreadsheet, then untick Page Breaks

Excel Security

It is possible to apply encryption to Excel spreadsheets, but it is riddled with issues. The focus of protection is on the spreadsheet's configuration rather than the details. One may attempt to lock certain sheets and cells to prevent users from modifying the layout & formula, but they can generally alter any of it if they see the data.

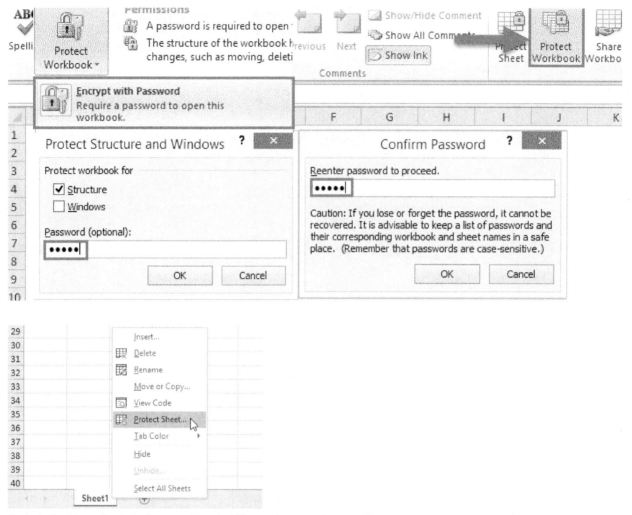

Switch the Enter key's influence. Excel shifts to the next down cell as one presses the Enter key. But what if one prefers to sit in the same cell? By using Tools, then Options, then Edit, one can make the Enter key carry them in either direction or keep them in the same cell.

CHAPTER 19: SHORT CUTS

51+ Excel Shortcuts You Need To Know

If you enter information on a daily basis in Excel or your employment requires that you use Excel at 100% of your working hours, it is essential that you know the Shortcuts in Excel. Shortcuts allow us to quickly access the icons and/or windows of all Excel tools from the keyboard, which will make us do everything faster.

In most cases, the shortcuts use the CTRL, Alt and Shift keys. The CTRL and Alt keys are always displayed on the keyboard with their name, while the Shift key is represented by an arrow and is known as "Shift."

With these shortcuts, you can perform the basic and essential tasks and move through the available options or tabs menus.

From there, you will have access to practically all the actions that Excel allows.

Excel Functions Keys

F1: Shows Excel help

F2: Enters edit mode for a selected cell

F3: If a name is specified, a "Paste name" dialog box is shown.

F4: Repeat the last action. In addition, writing a formula allows you to switch between relative, absolute and mixed references.

F5: Displays the Go to dialog box.

F6: Move between the panels of a divided book.

F7: Displays the Spelling dialog box.

F8: Activates the Expand selection mode that allows you to increase the selected range using the arrow keys.

F9: Calculate the result of the formulas of all the sheets of the open books.

F10: The menu bar is activated.

F11: The selected cell range is used to create a chart sheet.

F12: Displays the Save As dialog box.

Shortcuts of a Single Key

Alt: Activates the menu bar.

Page: Move one screen down inside the sheet.

Enter: Complete the entry of a cell and select the lower cell.

Esc: Cancels the entry of a cell. It also closes any dialog box shown.

Space: Activates or deactivates a check box within a dialog box.

End: Activates or deactivates the final mode. When in final mode, the arrow keys can be used to move to the last cell of the current range.

Page Up: Move one screen up inside the worksheet.

Backspace: Activates "Edit Mode" after deleting the contents of a cell.

Delete: Deletes the contents of a cell.

Tab: Complete the entry of a cell and select the cell on the right.

Direction keys: Select the upper, lower, left or right cell according to the pressed direction key.

Basic Keyboard Shortcuts in Excel

CTRL + U: New workbook.

CTRL + V: Insert, into the the selected cells, the clipboard's contents.

CTRL + X: Cut the selected cells.

CTRL + Y: Redoes the last undone action.

CTRL + Z: Undoes the last action.

CTRL + 1: With this command you can show the Format Cells dialog box.

CTRL + 2: Apply bold formatting to selected text.

CTRL + 3: Applies italic formatting to selected text.

CTRL + 4: Underline the selected text.

CTRL + 5: Applies the strikethrough effect to the text.

CTRL + 6: Hide or show sheet objects.

CTRL + 8: Displays the outline symbols on the sheet.

CTRL + 9: Hides the selected rows.

CTRL + 0: Hides the selected columns.

Shortcuts with Alt and Functions Keys

Alt + F1: Insert a chart in the current sheet.

Alt+F2: If you want to show the Save As dialog box, use this command.

Alt + F4: Close Excel.

Alt + F8: Opens the Macro dialog box.

Alt + F10: Displays the "Selection and visibility" panel for shapes.

Alt+F11: Use this command to get access the Applications Editor of Visual Basic.

Shortcuts with CTRL, Shift and Functions Keys

CTRL + Shift + F3: Displays the Create Names dialog box from what you have selected.

CTRL + Shift + F6: Go to the previous open workbook.

CTRL + Shift + F10: Activates the menu bar.

CTRL +Shift +F12: It display the Print dialog box.

CTRL + Shift + F: Displays the Source tab of the Format Cells dialog box.

CTRL + Shift + L: Enable or disable filters in a range.

CTRL +Shift +O: Use this command to choose cells with comments.

CTRL + Shift + U: Expand the formula bar.

CTRL + Shift + Enter: Enter a formula as a matrix formula.

CTRL + Shift + Start: Extends the selection to the beginning of the sheet.

CTRL + Shift + End: Extend the selection to the last cell used in the sheet.

CTRL + Shift + Page Down: Add the next sheet to the sheet selection.

CTRL + Shift + Page Up: Add the previous sheet to the sheet selection.

CTRL + Shift + Address key: Extends the selection to the last non-empty cell in the same direction as the key pressed.

CTRL + Shift + Space: Select the current cell range or the entire sheet.

CTRL + Shift + (:Shows hidden rows inside the specified cells range.

CTRL + Shift +) : Shows hidden columns inside the specified cells range.

CTRL + Shift +! : Apply the Number format with two decimals.

CTRL + Shift +$: The Currency format can apply with two decimals using this command.

CTRL + Shift +% : Applies the format Percent without decimals.

CTRL + Shift + / : Applies the Scientific notation format.

CTRL + Shift + : Applies the format category Time.

CTRL + Shift + & :This applies a border to the selected cell.

CTRL + Shift + - :Delete the selected cell borders.

CTRL + Shift +" :Copy the contents of the upper cell.

Keyboard Shortcuts to Move in Excel

Alt + Page: Move one screen to the right on the sheet.

Alt + Page: Move one screen to the left on the sheet.

CTRL +. : Move to the next corner of a selected range.

CTRL +Page: Switch to another or next sheet.

CTRL + Page: Move to the previous sheet.

CTRL + Start: Move to cell A1 or the upper left cell visible on the sheet.

CTRL + End: Move to the last cell used in the current range.

CTRL + Backspace: It shows the active cell by moving the screen.

CTRL + Tab: To go to the next open book.

CTRL + Direction key: Move to the end of the current row or column according to the pressed direction key.

Keyboard Shortcuts to Select Data

*CTRL + ***: Select the current region of cells with data.

CTRL + Space: Select the current column.

Shift +Page Down: You can down one screen while extend the selection.

Shift +Page Up: You can up one screen while extend the selection.

Shift + Start: Extends the selection to the beginning of the row.

Shift + Space: Select the current row.

Shift + Address key: Extends the selection one cell in the same direction as the key pressed.

Shortcuts to Enter Data and Formulas

Alt + = : Inserts an Autosuma from adjacent cells.

Alt + Down: Displays the options of a data validation list.

Alt +Enter: With this command, you can add a line break within a cell.

CTRL +, (comma): Insert the current date.

CTRL +: : Insert the current time.

CTRL + '(single quote): Copy and paste the top cell formula.

CTRL +Enter: The current entry can be filled the selected cell range using this command.

CTRL + Delete: Deletes all text until the end of the line.

CTRL + Alt + K: Insert a hyperlink.

Shift + Enter: Complete the cell entry and select the top cell.

Shift + Tab: Complete the cell entry and select the cell on the left.

Other Keyboard Shortcuts in Excel

Alt +Space: This command helps you to get access to the control menu of Excel sales.

Alt + ':(single quote) Displays the Style dialog box.

Alt + CTRL + Left : Moves to the left between non-adjacent cells of a selected range.

Alt + CTRL + Right : Moves to the right between non-adjacent cells of a selected range.

CTRL + - : Displays the Delete Cells dialog box.

CTRL ++ : The insert Cells dialog box can be shown by this command.

CTRL +Alt+ V: With this command, the Paste Special dialog box can be shown.

CONCLUSION

Congrats! In this book, we have delved deeper into Microsoft Excel. Microsoft Excel is, without a doubt, a challenging application to grasp and operate. That's why it is frequently advisable to enlist the help of others in figuring out how to cope with it efficiently. If you are a student who needs to know how to utilize Microsoft Excel to finish a school assignment, a businessperson who wants to expand their experience and learn new skills, or a person who wants to get a basic knowledge of Excel Spreadsheets for personal use, this book is appropriate for you. You may get a lot of high-quality visuals, tips, and techniques by going through this Microsoft Excel guide. You'll also get a comprehensive overview of all Excel essentials, allowing you to work with Microsoft Excel more comfortably on a daily basis. So you should give a chance to this book since it has all of the important facts.

Excel skills are some of those skills that have become very important in the job market today. They carry a lot of weight because Excel does not just represent one type of skill but a wide range of skills that employers are interested in so much. That is why people with good Excel skills stand a better chance of securing a job than those people who have little or no knowledge about the spreadsheet.

Excel skills will make things much easier for you in a job setting. You can, for instance, gather data easily if you are required to, analyze it if this is needed, and draw some conclusions from the data. Take your next Excel to extend and dissect it by experiencing each phase of this book; what's its motivation, structure, information passage, designing, and printing introduction.

Excel's main advantage is that it allows for speedy data input. MS Excel features a *Ribbon* interface, which is a collection of instructions that may be used to do particular tasks, as opposed to other data entering and analysis techniques.

Because Excel is part of the Microsoft Office suite, it may be able to connect with other apps in the suite. Microsoft Excel allows you to analyze, manage, and share data in further ways than it has ever been, assisting you in making better, more informed decisions. New data discovery and visualization applications make it easier to keep track of and show key data patterns.

Excel provides simple forms for people to collaborate on workbooks and improve the efficiency of their work. Best of all, users of older versions of Excel will always join without difficulty. Excel allows it easy to get what you need to be completed faster, with greater consistency and more performance.

Businesses are increasingly turning to cloud storage for data connectivity and collaboration. You will see Microsoft Excel's future over the next few years advancing at a breakneck pace to have multi-user access to vast data for research, monitoring, and significant improvements in performance and productivity.

Excel is often unavoidable in marketing, but with the tips mentioned above, it doesn't have to be so intimidating. Practice makes perfect, as they say. These formulae, shortcuts, and methods will become second nature the more you utilize them.

Printed in Great Britain
by Amazon

85553857R00106